Himalayan Mountain Cookery

A VEGETARIAN COOKBOOK

Compiled by
Martha Ballentine

with introductions and comments by
Rudolph M. Ballentine, M.D.

Published by

Himalayan International Institute
of Yoga Science and Philosophy of the U.S.A.
Honesdale, Pennsylvania 18431

© 1976 by The Himalayan International Institute
of Yoga Science and Philosophy of the U.S.A.
RD 1, Box 88
Honesdale, Pennsylvania 18431

Fourth Printing 1985

ISBN 0-89389-015-4

Library of Congress Cataloging in Publication Data

Ballentine, Martha, 1912—
    Himalayan Mountain cookery.

    Includes index.
    1. Cookery, Indic. 2. Cookery, Yoga. 3. Cookery—Himalaya Mountains Region.
4. Cookery, Vegetarian.
I. Title.
TX724.5.I4B27 1985 641.5954 84-29055

Contents

ॐ ब्रह्मार्पणां ब्रह्म हविः
ब्रह्माग्नौ ब्रह्मणा हुतम् ।
ब्रह्मैव तेन गन्तव्यं
ब्रह्म कर्म समाधिना ॥

Om Brahmar panam	The offering is to God.
Brahma havih	God is the offering.
Brahma agnau	The offering is made into the fire which is God.
Brahmana hutam	The offering is made by God.
Brahmaivatena gantavyam	God alone is the One to whom the offering is made.
Brahma karma samadhina	When seen through samadhi, all this action is of God.
Om visvatma priyatam	May the Universal Self be satisfied.
Om tat sat. Brahmar panam astu	That alone is true and real. The offering is to God.
Om shantih shantih shantih	Om peace peace peace

O God, bless this food so that it brings vitality and energy to fulfill Thy mission and serve humanity.

O God, bless this food so that we remain aware of Thee within and without.

O God, bless this food so that we love all and exclude none.

Bless those who have provided this food, who have prepared this food and who will eat this food.

Bless all, my Lord. Amen.

I

Introduction

Good on picnic!

Grape leaves in jar
Rinse well
vein side.
shiny side

Saute onion

2 cinnamon sticks

1/2 c rice long grain

little oil
thyme

3 T toasted pine nuts
· water   chop
                 fresh
let cook   mint
        or frozen blue 1/2 c
few currants raisins

Put filling on vein
                   side
fold tight

Put in pan
add. 1 1/4 c water or veg broth
lemon juice, boil
cover with parchment oiled
boil, let simmer 30 min til tender
      good hot or cold

Introduction

The Himalayan mountains contain the tallest peaks in the world. From high on these peaks the glaciers grind the soil, and melting snows carry down a rich supply of minerals to the farmlands below. The crops grown on the terraces of these mountains yield some of the best quality vegetables and grains known to man. From the deep valleys around the mountains up to the 25,000 foot peaks, almost every possible climatic condition exists. In the valleys are grown tropical fruits and vegetables, and on the high mountainsides the vegetation of the far north thrives. Within the space of a few miles one can find a variety of herbs, spices, vegetables, fruits, grains, beans and wild plants that is unmatched anywhere in the world. Over many thousands of years, in a tradition that is perhaps the most ancient in the world, the inhabitants of these mountains have selected and created for themselves a diet that is probably unparalleled in its nutritional qualities and its subtle flavors.

The people of the Himalayas are known throughout the world, and especially by the scientists of the West, for their incredible and enduring health. In many areas less touched by outside influences, they live vigorous and productive lives past the age of a hundred. They are known for their proud carriage, their tall stature, their handsome features, their intelligence and wisdom. Diseases that plague the people of the lowlands of India and the populations of the rest of the world are virtually unknown among the mountain people of the Himalayas. Their literacy and learning is profound, and it is not unusual to be surprised by a college or a university tucked away in a small town on a mountain slope. This is the center, too, of spiritual teachings, and the great philosophies of the East have flowed from these mountains for millennia. In isolated and little known monasteries high in the mountains the traditions of spiritual attainment continue.

In the monasteries and among the common people, the art of food preparation has been highly developed. Their hearty dishes, prepared for a cold climate, are well suited to the temperate and cooler parts of America and Europe and are more adapted to our vegetables, fruits and other crops than are the tropical dishes of Southern India. In the mountains there is a tradition of preparing food that is healthful, nourishing and hearty, and yet, at the same time, conducive to alertness and the practice of meditation.

From the mountain monasteries of India and Tibet, Swami Rama came to America to bring the insights of yoga science to the scientific and medical world. Having been raised in a monastery from the age of three, he also brought with him a long career of cooking mountain dishes and understanding of the relevance of food to health. He has been kind enough to share with us this knowledge of cooking and to teach us firsthand, through example, the methods that are used by the mountain folk. Each new dish is always more delightful than the last, and it is almost possible to say that Swamiji has never cooked the same thing twice. Once we have learned a recipe and find that we are able to carry it out, he always manages to leave us speechless by throwing in some totally unexpected and apparently incompatible ingredient, or picking up one pot which we have carefully prepared and dumping it into another, or adding "too much" of this or "not enough" of that. Yet each time there is a lesson to be learned, and surprisingly the results are, almost without exception, delicious.

If there is anything that can be learned from cooking with Swamiji, it is that cooking is a great art; perhaps the greatest. There are no hard and fast rules, and one must always proceed with a prayer on his lips and an openness to guidance from within. "I cook with love," Swamiji says, "and I cook for God. How can it not be good!"

A meal is prepared *for* someone or some people, *on* a certain day, *in* a certain season, according to the ingredients that are available. So it is quite impossible to pick up a recipe book and cook something from it. The finest art of cooking is always a matter of being sensitive to these things: the people for whom you're cooking, the weather, the climate, the time of the day, and using what is on hand, creatively and intuitively. There is perhaps no end to this learning; the more one practices and cooks, the sharper his sense of what is right and necessary becomes. As he is learning along the way, however, recipes from a master chef serve as a helpful guide. It is in this spirit that we offer the recipes that follow. Do not feel bound to them. Do not follow them slavishly; but learn from them, master them, and then gradually find your own way. Don't be "creative" beyond your capacity; the results can be disastrous. The great cook always warns, "Don't experiment with other people's stomachs."

It is hoped that with these recipes the public will be able to experience some of the delights of Himalayan Mountain cookery and benefit from the traditions and wisdom that have accumulated at "the top of the world" over thousands of years.

The Preparation of Food

Among the Brahmin families who live in the mountains and carry on the strictest traditions, the preparation of food is taken very seriously. It is the exclusive province of the wife of the family—both her sacred duty and her privilege. Brahmins are forbidden to eat food prepared by anyone but another Brahmin, since the care, the vibrations, the attention that goes into the food are considered to have a powerful effect on creating both the body and the mind of whoever partakes of it.

Before preparing a meal, the Brahmin woman bathes and puts on clean garments. She then enters the kitchen and begins the process of cooking as though she were performing a service of worship. With a serene mind and a mantra on her lips, she is constantly attentive to the nourishing of her family. If someone thoughtlessly enters the kitchen during this process, he is not only summarily thrown out, but so is the food, and she must start afresh.

Both in the home and the monastery waste is abhorred. Nothing is ignored and a proper place is always found for odd bits and pieces of ingredients. When they don't fit into one dish, there is always somehow a need for them in another. The scriptures say *"Annam Brahma"* which in Sanskrit means "in food there is some spirit, and it is alive."

II

Utensils and Cooking Oils

II Utensils & Cooking Oils

In the mountains, as elsewhere in India, cooking is often done out of doors. Here the utensils are solid, heavy and sturdy, and many dishes in the mountains are prepared by cooking directly on heated stones or otherwise in huge iron pots and woks. Great attention is given to both the cleanliness of the utensil as well as its composition. The material out of which the utensil is made can affect both the taste and the properties of the food. Thus it is that aluminum pots and pans are never used, and even brass and copper are not considered fit for cooking. Brass and copper are, on the other hand, highly prized for boiling water, and it is said that they purify it in the process.

Cooking utensils are ordinarily cast iron, pottery, steel, or—for the oldest traditional dishes—stones, leaves, or even the hot coals themselves.

When great attention is given to the subtleties of taste that are to be produced in a dish, then the exact shape and thickness of the bottom and walls of the pot in which it is cooked become very important. This is because the thickness and shape of the pot affect both the speed at which it cooks and the way in which the heat reaches the food, as well as the rapidity with which the moisture is lost.

In a thin pot the food will sear. The heat will affect that part in contact with the pot much more intensely than it affects the food in the center, which is far away from contact with the sides and bottom of the pot. This means that part of the food can easily scorch while the rest remains uncooked. In a thick, heavy pot, however, the heat is more evenly transmitted, and there is much less tendency for the food to scorch and stick to the bottom and sides. This does not mean that heavy pots should always be used; in fact, there are some dishes whose flavor depends entirely on their sticking to the sides of the pot, being scraped loose, and sticking again. Burning should never be permitted, or an unpleasant, bitter taste will result. But the slight roasting that results during the sticking of the food to the side of the pot gradually transforms the whole taste and flavor of the dish. More often, of course, a thick pot is useful, and it certainly requires less attention and stirring.

The shape of the vessel is probably at least as important as its thickness. In a deep pot which has straight sides there is relatively little surface area of the food being cooked which is in contact with the air. This means that the food will cook softer, it will be mushier and will not retain its shape and texture as well. The moisture will boil off more slowly, and the food is more nearly "trapped" in a boiling environment. When, by contrast, the sides of the vessel are sloped, as in the wok or *karhai* (as it is called in the Himalayas), the open surface area of the cooking food is much larger in comparison to its volume. This means that moisture is leaving rapidly, and it means that the food is more likely to retain its shape and less likely to cook apart. The wok, as it has come to be called in this country, is extremely important in cooking many mountain dishes.

A third shape which is very important is the skillet, or frying pan, where the sides are very low. For many of the dishes that are described herein it is important that the food be completely spread out and allowed to cook in contact with the hot cast iron surface, without being submerged in liquid or piled in on top of other chunks of food. For this purpose the best utensil is a large iron frying pan. "Large" means at least 14 inches in diameter, a size that is sometimes difficult to find in America. Such a pan, however, allows one to roast the vegetables in such a way as to develop a flavor that is quite unique and that is the basis of many of the delicious recipes in this book. A smaller iron frying pan can be used, of course, if one is only going to cook for a few people. In many cases, however, a 14 inch pan *filled* with vegetables will roast down to only enough to feed four or five.

A further reduction in the amount of moisture leaving the food can be produced by covering. When a lid is put on a pot or pan, the moisture is driven back into the cooking food; and this results in it becoming softer and more mushy. The extreme of such a procedure is the pressure cooker, where the lid is sealed and pressure builds up.

While certain techniques are necessary to prevent the food from becoming overcooked and losing its texture and flavor in a pressure cooker, it is nevertheless a highly useful and economic device, enabling one to cook rapidly many dishes that would otherwise require much time and fuel. Moreover, if properly used, it preserves the nutritional quality of the food, since much less of the nutrients are carried off in this method than leave with the steam during long hours of boiling. While the modern pressure cooker is a recent arrival in India, the practice of putting a huge stone on the lid of an iron pot is a time-honored procedure in Himalayan cookery.

Cooking Oils

The oils that are used for cooking vary from region to region in India, but in the mountains the favorite fat is *ghee,* a dairy product produced by boiling butter until the watery part disappears. When the solid material is thus removed, a clear liquid fat results which will solidify at room temperature. (See recipe on page 134.)

This "clarified butter," or *ghee* as it is called throughout India, is highly prized for its virtues. It is considered healthful, delicious and valuable, since it is both able to preserve foods and does not itself spoil. It can be kept for months at a time at room temperature without becoming rancid.

Ghee is particularly favored for cooking the herbs and spices before vegetables are added. This is because it can be heated to a high temperature without burning, whereas butter will scorch. Vegetable oils, by contrast, when heated to a high temperature are often damaged by this and become harmful.

Other oils highly favored in India for cooking are sesame oil and mustard oil. Mustard oil has a rather strong, pungent taste and should be used with discretion. Sesame oil is heavier and richer, and enjoys much popularity in China, also, where it is a frequent addition to Chinese vegetable dishes.

III

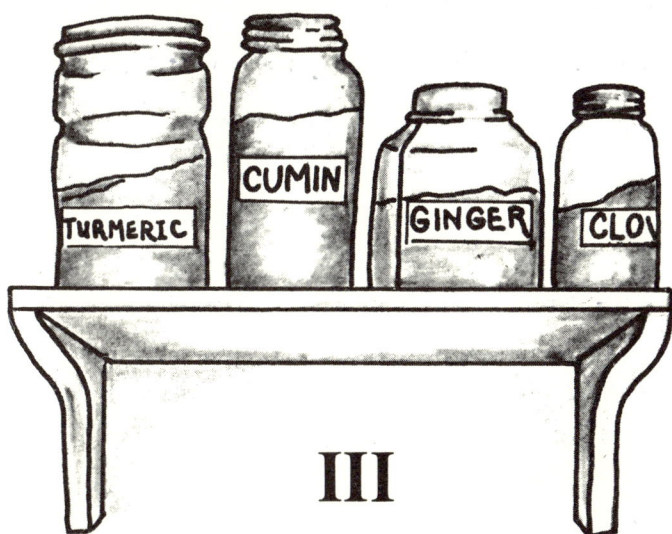

Spices and Herbs

Falasaid

Fava beans — remove from
pluck   pod

Kale -

Collards

beet greens

Broccolini — several minutes

Roast shole garlic — cut off parts
or kale   ends
cut across   wrap before
Boiling water   Bake 30 min
7 min   350
after blanched add to
In wok or pan pan — cooked short
oil add garlic . . .   Pasta Fuselli
hot pepper flakes . .
black pepper
add pasta

III Spices & Herbs

Indian dishes have a reputation for being highly spiced, but this is not universally so. In South India the food is extremely pungent, but in North India it is milder, and in the mountains less of the hot peppers are used.

Even in India, a good cook is considered to be one who uses spices not in excess, but with delicacy and subtlety, to complement the natural flavors of the food, to improve its digestibility, and to add healing and healthful properties to it.

The spices of India have been famed for centuries all over the world. Since the route through the Middle East to the East Indies was long, arduous, and fraught with dangers, spices brought extremely high prices, and were used as ransom and highly treasured. In the Middle Ages, when there were no facilities for refrigerating food, spices were used for their preservative qualities. They were thought to prevent spoilage, and modern research has borne this out. Sometimes, unfortunately, they were also used to cover up the taste of that which had already spoiled. Spices and herbs from the East were also valued for their medicinal properties. It is said that Columbus was regarded in his day, not as an adventurous explorer who discovered the new world, but as one who got lost while looking for a shorter way to get spices for the table of Isabella and Spain. Because of its rich supply of herbs and spices, India still supplies the raw materials for 80% of the world's natural (non-synthetic) medicines.

Each region in India has its favorite herbs and spices, which are to a large extent determined by what grows best in the local climate. On the steppes of the Himalayas, however, the whole spectrum of climatic conditions is present, and a variety of spices unequaled elsewhere is readily available. For this reason the mountains were long a center of knowledge about herbal medicines, as well as the point of origin of some of the most delicious dishes that the world has ever known. Their creation often depends on the proper selection and preparation of just the right amounts and combinations of herbs and spices.

For the Westerner, unfortunately, the spices that are added to most Indian food are often his greatest obstacle. He finds them irritating, and they create digestive problems, or he finds that they taste odd and unfamiliar. This is partly because the Indian food he has access to is often overspiced, and the spices are not used with discrimination. In this book we have endeavored to limit the use of spices to those which are most common, most mild and the most healthful. In so doing we are following the example set by the greatest mountain cooks.

In most vegetable, bean, and pea dishes the basic spices* are three: turmeric, cumin, and coriander.

Turmeric *(haldi)* Turmeric is the ground root of a plant that grows in India. It is bright yellow and has the power to create a most stubborn stain on clothes. It is best known to us in the West as an ingredient of prepared mustard, to which it gives a characteristic yellow color. (Mustard without turmeric is a drab beige color.) Sometimes it is also used by American cooks to flavor pickles and relishes. Turmeric has been highly regarded by health-conscious groups who reject most spices (for example the Seventh Day Adventists), and in India has long been considered very valuable in curing and preventing many diseases, such as diabetes and cancer. Research is underway in India now to look into the validity of this belief, and initial results seem to indicate that turmeric does have some value in these areas. It is also famous in the East for its effects on the skin, and it is often said by the traditional doctors of India that the women there owe their beautiful complexions to the daily consumption of turmeric in the diet. In fact, it is rare to encounter an Indian dish that

---

* In fact it is not really correct to call these *spices;* they are more accurately termed *herbs,* being primarily mild and of great value in preventing illness and promoting digestion.

doesn't contain some turmeric, and it seems to the foreigner that the Indian cook is always tossing turmeric in one thing or another. Its flavor is best when it is well cooked. When the herbs and spices are added to the fat at the beginning of preparation of an Indian dish, turmeric should be added first, so that it may cook longest.

Cumin *(jeera)* Cumin has been known in the West since antiquity and was mentioned in both the Bible and the works of Hippocrates. In the Middle Ages in Europe it was a very popular culinary herb. It has long been valued both there and throughout the world for its ability to promote digestion and to reduce gas. In the Southwest United States it is traditionally added to pinto beans to aid their digestion, and it is a frequent companion to beans and peas of all sorts throughout the world. To most Americans it is familiar as a major constituent of chilli powder, giving it its characteristic flavor. In India it is even used to make a drink called *Jaljeera* (cumin water), which is taken after the meal to aid in digestion. Yet of these three basic herbs it is probably the most irritating and strongest in taste, and newcomers to Indian food who have no experience with cumin may wish to begin by using it in very small quantities. (Usually the basic recipes for vegetables or main dishes contain twice as much cumin as turmeric.) Cumin is used either whole or ground, and though the flavor is much the same, a different effect is produced. When the cumin seeds are added to the frying fat which already contains turmeric, they should be allowed to roast and cook until they begin to turn brown and split open. Otherwise, their full-bodied flavor and aroma will not develop.

Coriander *(dhania)* Coriander is the herb that is used in our mountain cookery in the largest quantities. Whereas one part of turmeric is used and two parts cumin, three parts of coriander are almost always added. It is said that coriander counteracts the unpleasant effects of cumin and complements it nicely. Moreover, coriander, on its own, is one of the most highly regarded herbs ever used by man. It is said in the ancient medical scriptures of India that it has the power to improve any diseased state that exists. Among the Seventh Day Adventists in America, it is highly recommended. The rural people of many sections of America have prized it highly, and it is added in large quantities to such favorite foods as sausage and apple pie. It has a pleasant and agreeable taste, and is not toxic, even in large quantities. It is said that the inhabitants of Peru, where another highly evolved mountain culture developed, are so fond of the taste and smell of coriander that it is used in almost all of their dishes. In Egypt, as well as in India, leaves of the fresh plant are used, as well as the ground coriander to which we here refer. It is said that the seeds have a disagreeable taste on gathering, but that the longer they are kept the more fragrant they become. Of course, eventually they will lose their fragrance as it dissipates into the air. Though it comes originally from the East, it has been known in Europe and the West since the time of the Greeks and Romans. It has been used in Britain and America in medicines, primarily to cover up the unpleasant taste of other ingredients. It is also said to be good for digestion and helpful in reducing gastrointestinal gas. Coriander develops a delicious flavor when fried until brown, and then when liquid is added, it helps to thicken the sauce of a vegetable or dahl, creating a gravy-like effect.

Below is a description of other herbs and spices that are used in Indian cooking. However, they are not as common in our recipes, or as highly regarded as the three above, which are the most healthful, valuable, and universally used.

Mustard Seed *(rai ka bij)* In Western cooking, yellow mustard seeds are used. Generally, except for use in pickles, they are ground and made into the familiar prepared mustard that we spread on bread to make sandwiches. In India, however, yellow mustard seeds are not used for this purpose; they are only used for making oil. For cooking, black mustard seeds are used, which are considered to be more flavorful. When used in cooking, they should be added after the basic spices and allowed to fry until they begin to pop, but not explode like popcorn.

Black Pepper *(kali mirch)* Black pepper is not so universally used in Indian cooking as it is in the West, but it is nevertheless highly regarded and is a frequent addition to certain dishes. It does not require the kind of frying that other spices do and can be added later in the preparation. It is also very effective in promoting digestion, reducing gas, and helps to reduce the tendency to form mucus.

Red Pepper *(lal mirch)* Red pepper, or cayenne, is a much abused spice in Indian cooking, as it is in Mexico, where it originated. Introduced to India from the West, it came to replace black pepper and a native Indian pepper called *pippali,* which was used to give the pungent taste to Indian dishes. Red pepper is often used in great quantities, which causes much irritation of the stomach and bowels. This overuse is probably due to its high quantity of vitamin C, which makes it much valued by poorer people whose diet is deficient in fresh vegetables and fruits. The red pepper also serves to offset the mucus-forming properties of a primarily starchy diet. When used in small quantities, occasionally, it can complement a dish nicely.

Fenugreek *(methis)* This is a little cube-shaped seed which has a delightful maple-like flavor. It is often used to give a maple flavor to candies and other commercial products. In India the leaves are cooked as a vegetable, and fenugreek is a common ingredient in prepared curry powder, where it is combined with turmeric, cumin, and other common spices. If it is used in too large a quantity, it gives a bitter taste; but in small amounts it adds a pleasant mapleish flavor to the dish.

Ginger *(adarak)* Fresh ginger is often used in dahls and vegetables and is very delicious if the roots are in good condition. It is usually grated or pounded until it is a paste, and then this is fried in the ghee along with the other spices. Ginger is very pungent, or hot, and usually cannot be left in large pieces because it will irritate the mouth and intestines. It is very good for adding a warming quality to foods in the cold weather, and is treasured for its ability to reduce mucus. A chunk of ginger is often thrown into the pot with boiling water for tea in the winter time. Dried ginger may be stored as a whole root, but when time comes for it to be used, it is ground. Powdered, dried ginger can be found easily in grocery stores, but should be checked to make sure that it is still fragrant and fresh. After it sits for more than a couple of months, it loses its good taste and its beneficial properties and should be discarded.

Black Cardamom These are different from the cardamoms that are available in American supermarkets; they are larger and darker. The big, black cardamom is used to flavor vegetables, whereas the small, light cardamom is used in desserts and sweet dishes. Black cardamom has a stronger and odder taste, but sometimes lends a nice twist to the flavor of a vegetable dish.

Cinnamon Cinnamon is one of the Indian spices which is familiar to the Westerner, and it also may be one of the oldest. Cinnamon is basically the bark of a tree, and this bark can be bought in rolled-up dried strips or powdered. The quality of cinnamon varies widely with the spices of the tree and where it is grown. One should always be careful to check cinnamon when buying it to make sure that it's what one had in mind. A dash of cinnamon is used in some Indian dishes and gives them a unique flavor. The variety that grows in India is more suited to vegetable dishes and is not used in sweets.

Cloves Cloves are another Indian spice familiar in the West. Cloves are used in making Indian vegetable dishes, rather than sweets. The clove has a very strong taste and is very powerful, so it should be used only in tiny quantities.

Saffron Saffron is the most precious of all spices. A tiny amount (a few grams) are stuffed in a cellophane envelope and put in the usual spice jar to sell in the supermarket. The reason it is so expensive is because it is only the yellow stigmas plucked from a crocus flower, and many thousands of flowers are necessary to make an ounce. It is cultivated in Spain and

Kashmir. A tiny amount makes a deep yellow color; according to tradition, the robes of swamis were once dyed with this saffron color. Nowadays it's difficult to obtain pure saffron because the pistils of the safflower are used as a substitute or adulterant, though the safflower is in no way related to saffron and does not have the fine taste. Saffron is used both for sweet dishes and often for coloring and flavoring rice.

Cassia *(tej pat)* This is the leaf of the Indian variety of cinnamon tree. It is used much as bay leaves are used in the West, and often Indian cooks in Western countries will substitute the bay leaf. However, there is a difference, for the *taj pat* has a delicate zest that can transform tomato soup from a common dish into an aristocratic delicacy. It is also ground and used in *garam masala* (prepared hot curry powders; see below).

Ajwain This is a seed of the same family as cumin, fennel, caraway and anise. It is tinier and rounder and has a distinctive flavor that is much favored as an addition to certain breads, and occasionally in the preparation of vegetables. In India it is sometimes called "king's cumin," but it does not seem to be available in the West.

Garlic Garlic is often used in vegetables as part of the seasoning; but we have not included it in recipes in this book since it is offensive to many people and too harsh for others. Its medicinal properties, however, may sometimes be useful.

Asafoetida *(hing)* This is another Indian spice which is very strong and has potent medicinal properties. For this reason we have eliminated it from all recipes. It is the resin from a tree that grows primarily in Persia and, if included in the diet of those who are not accustomed to it, will often produce diarrhea.

Most of the herbs and spices listed above need some cooking before they can be used in a dish. For this reason it is customary to start the preparation of an Indian dish by putting a small amount of fat in a frying pan and frying the spices in it for a certain amount of time. Vegetables are then added afterwards, usually the onions first. This is not an inviolable rule, however, and sometimes turmeric, cumin and coriander are simply dumped into the boiling pot of food and allowed to cook along with everything else. However, it is the length of time that the spices are fried which brings out the flavors that give each dish its uniqueness, and while one may sometimes find it a pleasant change to simply cook the spices along with the food, this will quickly become monotonous. Moreover, it lacks the rich roasted flavor that frying can give. Certain spices like red or black pepper should not be fried very much, and if red pepper is fried at a high temperature it will develop a most offensive odor.

Spices can also be roasted without fat in a dry pan, and this is sometimes done for certain dishes. This gives yet another flavor and provides another dimension for creative seasoning.

It should be noted that the fried herbs, especially turmeric and coriander, serve as the base for sauces that eventually result during the cooking of an Indian vegetable. The way in which they are prepared will determine their flavor and therefore will determine the "kind of sauce" in which the vegetable is served.

There are a number of prepared curry powders or *masalas* which are available in Indian stores even in this country. They are usually a combination of turmeric, cumin and coriander with often fenugreek, red pepper, mustard seed, ginger and sometimes others of the spices listed above. One cannot determine, however, the appropriate proportions of spice for each dish by using these, and more often they may contain ingredients one would rather avoid. In addition, they are sometimes not as fresh as one might wish.

It is very important that the herbs and spices used in Indian cooking be very fresh. For this reason we sometimes keep the whole cumin seed or coriander seed and grind them before using. Even whole turmeric roots will keep better than the ground turmeric, but usually enough of it is sold so that there is a rapid turnover, and what is bought is usually fresh, even in American supermarkets. The less frequently used spices, however, which might sit on the shelf for some time, will gradually lose their flavor and should be bought whole and ground before use. Even then one must be careful, since they may have been gathered many months or years before. The best rule of thumb is that a spice in its whole form, such as a seed or root, will keep up to six months and sometimes more. After it is ground, however, it will usually lose its flavor within two or three months.

There are a number of spices and flavorings which are used primarily for sweet dishes. White cardamom is one of these and has a very fine, delicate taste. If, however, it is not fresh, it will have a strong offensive flavor and be quite reminiscent of cough syrup (of which it is one of the major ingredients). Saffron, of course, is also commonly used for sweet dishes, and fortunately only the tiniest bit is necessary. Rose water, which is made by distilling a mixture of rose petals and water, has a very delicate flavor and is sometimes used in flavoring sweets. It too, however, will not keep indefinitely, and bottles of rose water should be checked, since they will often grow mold.

There are a few spices and herbs which are used to nibble on after a meal. They are said to promote digestion, and are quite refreshing and pleasant, a delightful substitute for a heavy sweet dessert. The favorite among these are cardamom, white cardamom and *saunf* (something between anise and fennel). One cardamom can be opened and the little black seeds inside chewed individually, providing up to a half hour of entertainment for your taste buds. The *saunf* seeds are often roasted and develop a very rich taste which is both pleasant and a great aid in digestion and the prevention of gas. It is not uncommon for the Indian host or hostess to pass around a tiny silver or glass tray containing little piles of these spices for one to enjoy after dinner.

IV

Basic Plan
for a Balanced Meal

Rice paper wrappers
stuff with

Peanut Sauce

IV Basic Plan
for a Balanced Meal

When they first begin to eliminate meat from their diet, many people find themselves confused and somewhat frightened about getting a truly balanced diet. In a culture where menu planning is centered around meat, there is little understanding of how to combine the various non-meat foods to assure good nutrition. In the Himalayas, however, where vegetarianism has been predominant for thousands of years, the understanding of sound meal planning is part of traditional training.

For example, the combining of a legume (bean or pea) with a grain (such as rice or bread) is a longstanding tradition in central Asia, as it is in most parts of the world. This forms, in a sense, the core of the meal, but one other component of the menu is equally important in insuring adequate nutrition. That is a vegetable dish, usually, at least in part, green. Because the mountain people are lacto-vegetarians in large part, that is, they use milk products, a milk-based dish such as yogurt is often also a prominent item on the menu and contributes to nutritional soundness.

A typical meal, then, will include the following:

1. **Rice** The rice is preferably only lightly milled after being parboiled as is the case with basmati rice (or completely unmilled as is the case with the mountain red rice). Rice is most often prepared plain, that is, only cooked in water with no salt or any other ingredient added. It serves, then, as a very bland base into

which the other spicier or more flavorful items in the meal are mixed. Usually, the pile of rice or the bowl of rice is put in the center of the plate from which one eats. Then, a little bit of the *dahl* (bean or pea) dish may be spooned onto the rice for one taste treat, whereas later some of the vegetable dish may be used likewise. This provides a variety of tastes and combinations, with the rice always serving as the mild staple that is combined with the stronger dahl or vegetable.

2. **Bread** Bread is also cooked without salt and usually without any additions, although there are exceptions to this (see recipes for breads). The msot common form of bread, of course, is the *chapati,* which is nothing more than flour and water with no fat, leavening, salt, flavoring or any other ingredient. The *chapati,* like rice, is a very bland base which complements nicely the more flavorful and zesty dishes that are made from dahl and vegetables. Not all the breads are made from wheat flour; other grains such as *bajara* (black millet) or *makkai* (corn or maize flour) may be used. In the West, a very good whole grain loaf bread which is yeasted and raised (called in India *double roti),* can be sliced and toasted and provides a very nice substitute for the flat breads *(rotis)* such as *chapati.* Either rice or bread may be used according to one's taste or to what is available. However, for a large, hearty meal, both are usually included.

3. **Dahl** (Beans, peas, lentils, etc.). The beans or peas (dahl preparations) are almost universally served with rice and bread as a way of creating a wholesome vegetarian protein which contains all the essential amino acids. In India this is done by cooking the dahl in a broth, which makes a rather thin, gravy-like substance that can be ladled onto the rice or into which the bread can be dipped. The dahl is always very well cooked until it is quite soft (in fact, cooks apart), and spices and seasonings are added to increase its digestibility, since beans and peas are notorious for causing intestinal gas. This problem is avoided through proper preparation and by serving only a small bowl of dahl, which is then used in relatively small proportions as compared to

the other items on the menu.

4. Vegetables This is the most vibrant and vitamin-packed item on the Indian menu and is universally prepared from freshly picked vegetables which come out of the home garden or which are purchased from a marketplace where they were brought from the fields on that very day. Because of the hot climate that prevails in most parts of India and even in the mountains during midday, vegetables keep very briefly. So, those picked in the morning are purchased before evening, and it is this which assures their freshness and nutritional value. Green vegetables are the most highly prized and certainly the most nutritionally valuable. They are often combined with, or used in alternation with, such vegetables as summer squash, carrots, green peas, okra, string beans, and so forth. Spinach and mustard greens are very important ingredients. Unfortunately, the less healthful vegetables, such as potatoes, eggplant and cauliflower, are cheaper in India and are often used in larger proportions or to substitute for other vegetables. When this is done, it is usually out of economic necessity, and most people realize the value of, and prefer, the green and yellow and less starchy vegetables.

5. Yogurt A very frequent addition to the above basic meal is a dish of yogurt, which is usually spiced with pepper and cumin or some other seasoning and may be combined with fresh cucumber or other salad-like vegetables. This produces something like a fresh salad with a yogurt dressing, though there is more dressing than salad, the purpose being to increase the amount of milk in the diet and boost the nutritional value of the meal. *Paneer* or fresh cheese made from milk curdled with lemon juice is often combined with the vegetables, in which case the yogurt may be omitted from the meal. But, the spiced yogurt salad dish is often pleasant to eat, complementing nicely the other items on the menu and cooling one's mouth after a spicy vegetable or dahl. The yogurt, of course, also provides the proper intestinal bacteria and is, for many reasons, a valuable addition to the diet.

6. **Chutney** An optional item on the menu is chutney, a sort of relish or pickle which is often prepared from fresh vegetables, such as green pepper, tomatoes, onion, and so forth. These fresh, pungent vegetables are chopped together and served in small spoonfuls as a zesty side dish to spice up the meal and stimulate the appetite and digestion. It is also, of course, a convenient way to sneak in fresh vegetables such as peppers and tomatoes, which contain high quantities of vitamin C. Chutneys can be hot or mild, depending on the kind of peppers and ingredients that are used.

These, then, are the basic items in any typical Indian meal, and probably two-thirds of all meals served in India include these basic dishes whenever possible. There are many varied and complex ways of preparing each of these items, such as rice dishes which include peas, vegetables, spices, nuts, etc., or breads which require the addition of spices and vegetables, deep frying and so forth. The basic preparation of these items need not be complicated, and they can each be put together in a short time if they are done in a plain and simple fashion.

Simple, everyday methods of preparing the basic items in an Indian meal are as follows:

a. *Dahl* (Beans, peas, lentils and so forth.) In the mountains, moong dahl (mung beans) is most commonly used. The beans may be used either whole or split. When split, the green covering may be either left on or removed. After carefully removing debris and pebbles, the dahl is cooked in water, usually about four or five times as much water as dahl. Meanwhile, the basic spices (usually turmeric, cumin and coriander in proportions of one, two and three parts) are fried in oil or fat, such as ghee. Other spices and herbs may be added as one wishes, and then onions are chopped or sliced and fried until limp. By this time, the dahl should be soft enough to mash between the fingers, and the spices, onions and salt are mixed with it. More water may be added if necessary. It is then cooked until it is the right soupy consistency. (For details and more elaborate recipes, see Chapter VII.)

b. **Rice**   Rice must be picked over, especially the rices that come from India which have not been commercially processed. This means that the grains which still have the husks on (this is different from bran) must be removed, along with any debris or pebbles, as with dahl. The rice is then rinsed in cold water till the water is clear, then put into a pot with enough water to cover the rice to about the second finger joint. No salt or anything else is added. The rice is brought to a rolling boil and the heat is then turned to the lowest flame. The pot is covered and allowed to cook without being stirred until all the water is absorbed and it is fluffy. (For rice recipes, see Chapter VI.)

c. **Vegetables**   The basic Indian vegetables are prepared by simply cutting them up in bite-size pieces and stir-frying in a wok or iron frying pan. Before the vegetables are added, the three basic herbs and spices (turmeric, cumin and coriander in proportions of one, two and three) are fried in a little ghee or other fat. The vegetables may then be added, those that require the longest cooking first, though usually onions are cooked well before anything else. If the vegetables are not watery, water may have to be added and then they are cooked until quite tender (for details on individual recipes, see Chapter V).

d. **Breads** The basic bread is *chapati* and this is prepared by simply kneading flour and water until a nice, springy dough is produced. Walnut-sized pieces are broken off and rolled out as thin or thick as taste dictates. These are cooked on a dry griddle until slightly brown and then thrown directly onto the flames for an instant or two until they puff up. Then they are buttered and served hot. Though simple and quick, if the flour is fresh and they are properly prepared, they are both tender and fragrant and add a substantial, chewy texture which other parts of the meal may lack. (In the Western kitchen a hearty whole grain toast may be substituted.)

e. **Yogurt** This may be served plain in a little bowl or honey can be stirred in. For spicier dishes, seasoning like black pepper and roasted cumin are added and fresh vegetables such as cucumber may be chopped and stirred in.

f. **Chutney** This optional part of the meal is prepared in India by grinding with a stone various peppers, tomatoes and so forth. In the West, a blender is a great time saver and green peppers, tomatoes, a little spinach or coriander leaves (or parsley, if you wish) and a touch of raw onion may be dumped in the blender and chopped to produce a nice relish-like consistency. A spoonful of this somewhere on the plate is a pleasant surprise and adds a little zip to the meal.

These are, of course, only the basic recipes for the simplest possible version of each of these components of the typical Himalayan meal. There are many, many variations, some of which are extremely complex and elaborate. For a basic, everyday meal, however, this is all that is necessary.

In fact, the preparation of the meal can be made even

simpler. The basic components need not be cooked separately. For instance, rice and dahl are often cooked together. This combination is called *khichari* and is a favorite in India (as in many other parts of the world). It is also handy for the cook who only has one big pot left or no more room on the stove.

Another shortcut is to cook together the vegetables and dahl (see recipes on page 98). Though usually the dahl will require some precooking, this still is a simplified way of preparing these two components, since only one pot is used and serving is simplified. The quickest adaptation in the West is to cook the dahl in the pressure cooker, open it, throw in the vegetables and then bring to pressure again (see recipe on page 52).

There are even one-pot dishes for open fire or a single burner stove, such as *Fakir Ki Khichari* ("The Wandering Monk Khichari," see page 85) which includes rice, dahl and vegetables, all cooked together in one pot. This can be a disaster if you don't know what you are doing. However if it is properly prepared, it turns out a light and delicious meal which is adequate unto itself and becomes a banquet when served with toast or *chapati*.

The addition of the dairy dish in the meal (yogurt or cottage cheese) is not as essential as the above ingredients (grain, vegetable and dahl). However, it is pleasant to have the dairy dish from time to time and it gives a considerable boost nutritionally to the meal.[1] There are other ways of including the yogurt, however, such as *karhi*, which is a combination of vegetables, gram flour (a dahl) and yogurt. This is served with rice and sometimes bread and, therefore, all the components of the basic meal are present in two (or three) simple dishes.

Of course, many other combination dishes are used in India, but these are the most common and this, at least, will convey the idea that *one need not prepare four or five separate*

---

[1] The milk is a source of vitamin B_{12} which may be absent in the strictly vegetarian items on the menu. Of course, only a tiny amount of B_{12} is needed and if yogurt is included in the meal every few days, this would be adequate.

items to produce a balanced meal as long as he includes the four or five basic ingredients in some combination.

Once the cook grasps the basic plan of the Indian meal and understands these essential components, he can easily modify his menu according to what groceries are on hand, what pots and pans and utensils are available and the tastes of the people whom he will feed. Though many detailed recipes are given later in the book for various kinds of dahl, various kinds of vegetables, various rice dishes and different breads, they are given as illustrations, rather than recipes to be slavishly followed. If one uses this book for some time, he should acquire a feel for the taste, texture and nutritional balance of Himalayan Mountain cooking and gradually learn to create his own dishes out of what is available, following the basic principles outlined.[1]

[1] For more details see *Diet and Nutrition* by Rudolph Ballentine, M.D., published by the Himalayan International Institute, Honesdale, Pennsylvania.

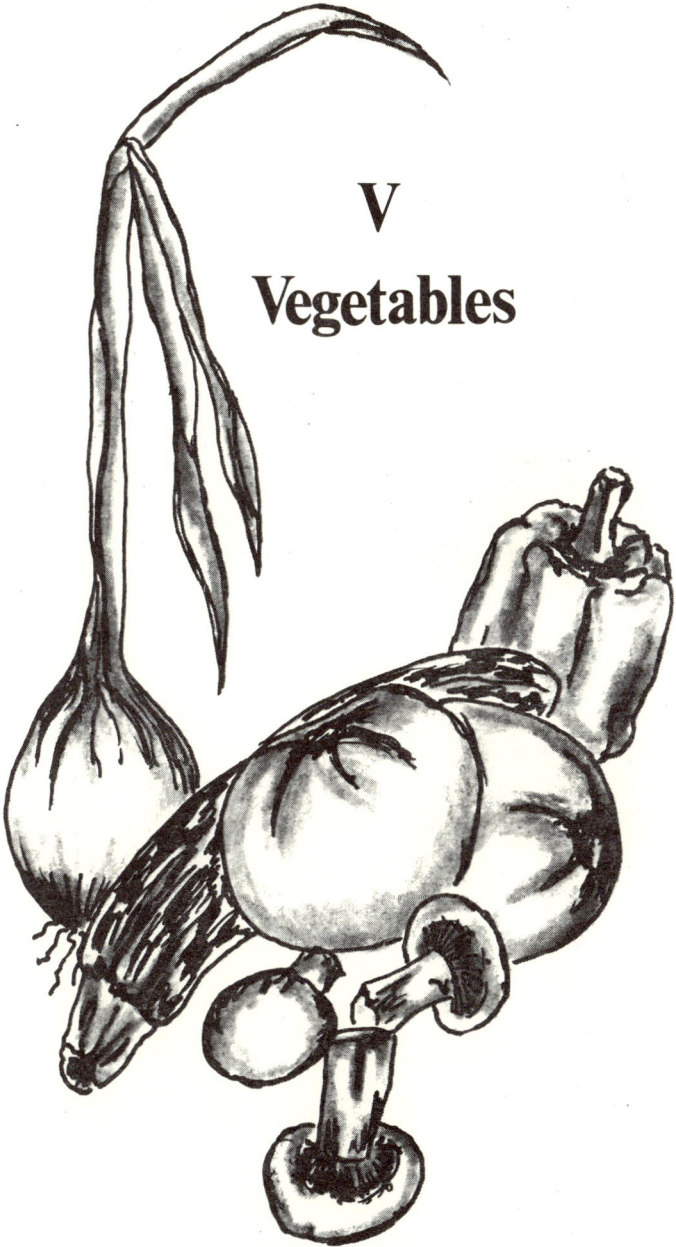

V
Vegetables

V. Vegetables

Vegetables are the heart of the Indian meal. A typical healthful Indian meal would consist of rice, dahl, perhaps a yogurt dish, usually with bread of some sort, and, last but not least, a vegetable dish. The vegetable is perhaps the most concentrated dish in the whole meal. This is because of a variety of vegetables. Especially green vegetables are selected and "cooked down" until the small dish of vegetable which is finally served contains perhaps the equivalent of three or four times as many vegetables as in their uncooked fresh state. Moreover, none of the water is thrown away and none of the essence of the vegetables is lost. It is concentrated. It is perhaps true that some of the nutrients are lost in the process of cooking, but the vegetables are made more digestible, too.

A variety of spices is used in the preparation of Indian vegetables. The exact spices used and their amount will vary incredibly from one part of India or one part of the Himalayan area to another. They will even vary considerably from person to person depending on who's doing the cooking.

The basic process of cooking an Indian vegetable is very straightforward and simple. There are many variations, and these can be woven around the basic process, once it is mastered. If the vegetables are cooked properly, they will be whole, retaining their shape, and will be blended so that the sauce or gravy that results contains a unique taste while each of the vegetables retains its own character. The important factors are the kind of pan that the vegetable is cooked in, how long it is cooked at each stage before a new ingredient is added, what spices are used, and how long they are cooked, whether it is covered or not, and for how long, and so forth. These variables are more important in the final outcome and taste of the vegetable, perhaps, than the ingredients themselves. At least four or five dishes which are completely different and unique can be prepared from exactly the same ingredients.

Cooking these vegetables requires patience, attention and love. With time and care, one can come to turn out masterpieces from the simplest of vegetable ingredients that will delight the most discriminating palate. When unobscured by excessive oil or hot chillis, the exquisite aromas and flavors of Indian vegetables cannot be matched by any dish prepared anywhere else in the world.

The first helpful hint for the cook is to prepare all the ingredients and have them ready before he begins. If someone is helping him, he need not worry about this.

Following are the steps in preparing a vegetable. By using this process, one can prepare a delicious dish from whatever vegetables he has on hand providing he has a few basic ingredients:

1. Into a large iron frying pan, put two or three tablespoons of ghee, turn the heat on medium and let the ghee begin to get hot. (A 10-inch frying pan is big enough to cook for two or perhaps three people; if you wish to cook for four to six, you need a 12 to 14-inch pan.) Meanwhile, add approximately a teaspoon of turmeric (this is for two to four people in a 10 to 12-inch pan), and between one and two teaspoons of cumin whole or ground or combination; then add about two to three teaspoons of ground coriander. (Black mustard seed, about a teaspoon or less, is an optional addition. If used, put in towards the end of browning and stop frying when the seeds begin to pop.) Keeping the heat at medium and stir, let these spices brown. The cumin seed should become brown. The spices can be

cooked either until browning begins or until they are quite dark brown or almost black. This will have a great deal to do with the flavor of the vegetable. There is no right or wrong way—only what is appropriate for the vegetable that's being cooked.

2. Add about two medium or small onions which have been sliced in rings about 3/8-inch thick; stir these as they brown and turn translucent. (Onions may be omitted for those who dislike them.)

3. Add chunks of bell pepper or fresh mushrooms or both, letting these cook for a few minutes. The heat should be on medium to medium-high so that the vegetables sizzle.

4. Add green vegetables, e.g., asparagus, broccoli, zucchini, string beans, and so forth. It is very important not to put too many vegetables in the pan. The vegetables should be spread out. They should fry in the spices and ghee so that the outside is somewhat seared.

5. Add water or cover, letting the natural juice come out of the vegetables. At the same time, add salt.

6. Cook covered for some time and then uncovered for some time, alternating according to whether the vegetables look as though they are getting soft. If they look as though they might begin to cook apart, uncover; if they look as though they are not cooking and are remaining tough, then cover. Sometimes the soft vegetables like zucchini may cook apart while others retain their shape. That is all right, but they shouldn't all be mushy.

7. If one wishes, toward the end of the cooking, additional ingredients can be added. Fresh tomatoes, peeled and pureed, can be poured in just enough to cover the top, letting them gradually cook into the mixture without stirring. Milk may be added instead of water when the water begins to dry up, or tomato can be added, and then later milk. This will give a very delicious broth to the vegetables. Cooked, split mung beans, cooked whole mung beans, or any other dahl can also be poured in at this point. The amount of tomato, milk, or dahl added should not be more than one-third of the volume in the pan.

8. The vegetables may require up to an hour to cook, if something like string beans are included. If the vegetables are softer, they will be done quicker.

9. The vegetables are done when the ghee begins to ooze out, forming a film on the top of the vegetable. At that point, the vegetables are "giving up their heart" or essence and are ready to be served. The cook should allow enough moisture to cook out of the vegetable at this time, so that it reaches the correct consistency. It can be cooked down dry enough to be served on a plate or it can be left in a soupy broth. Which is most appropriate will depend on the kind of vegetable used and the effect desired.

That is the basic method. Using it, one can toss in almost anything if he keeps in mind the taste and is sure that it will be compatible with what he has already begun with. For a traditional vegetable of the mountain variety, however, the basic ingredients should remain onions, mushrooms and green vegetables.

The vegetables can be cooked by adding water, or the water can be left out. If no water is put in, then they have to be covered more often, and this is only possible when very watery vegetables like zucchini are used. If only relatively dry vegetables like asparagus, string beans and broccoli are used, then water will have to be added. If there is a preponderance of zucchini, tomatoes, or leafy green vegetables which will wilt and lose their water, then it is possible to cook the whole vegetable without adding water. When this is possible, it is very desirable since it produces a wonderfully delicious taste and very likely damages the vegetables much less.

The taste of the vegetable is very much dependent on whether it is cooked open, covered, or cooked in a pressure cooker. Cooking the vegetables open the whole time will produce a meatier, chewier, firmer consistency, and the flavor will be richer and more roasted. If the vegetables are covered, they become softer and milder, and when they are cooked in a pressure cooker, they are extremely mild to the point of being bland, unless one is careful.

The same thing applies to stirring the vegetables and adding water. If they are constantly covered with water, then they tend to cook apart and become soft. For this reason, it is important to let the water cook away, fry them a bit, add more water, and repeat this several times. If the vegetables are covered with water, and it seems as though they might be cooking apart too softly, then it is a good idea to heap them up in mounds, allowing the water to run between them in "canals." An old swami in the mountain monasteries commented that it was quite impossible to learn to cook properly without knowing the "canal method."

Another important trick in producing a vegetable which is delicious and tasty is to allow the bottom to "candy." This means that during the long cycle of cooking, there will be, frequently, times when the vegetable "sticks" to the bottom of the frying pan. If it is allowed to remain too long and burns, it will give a bad bitter taste to the vegetable. If it is scraped away too quickly, however, the vegetable will remain bland and never develop any flavor. This sediment should be allowed to stick just long enough to roast and brown a bit; then it should be scraped loose and the process repeated. This is carried on primarily during the time when the water has cooked out and before new water is added. This is a very important facet to cooking the vegetable, and mastering this will enable one to turn out a variety of tastes each of which is more delicious than the last.

By properly altering the time that the vegetables are covered, the length of cooking, the amount of water added, the intervals at which it is added, and the spices and the vegetables used as ingredients, one can produce a wide variety of flavors and tastes. In our kitchen, we have cooked dishes which could easily pass for "fish," "gumbo," "turkey soup," "beef stew," or "game birds smothered in gravy." In each case, we could have easily passed these off to non-vegetarians as their favorite meat dishes—and in some cases, we did!

Cooking Indian vegetables should be a constant process of

experimentation, but like all good experiments, it should never wander too far from what is already known. The basic process should be followed and modifications gradually introduced as one has the feeling and confidence of what is appropriate. Totally "original creations" may satisfy your ego but do violence to the stomachs of those for whom you are responsible. For the sake of guiding those who are beginning, we have provided the series of recipes that follow. The theme above will be found running through these. The basic process is very similar; these are only modifications. Try them once you have felt that you have understood and have the feeling for them, then begin to create your own dishes.

The mountain style vegetables described here are one of the most concentrated forms of vitamins, minerals and proteins known to the diet of man. Leafy vegetables should be added when available since after they cook down and become soft, they are both digestible and incredibly nutritious. They contain extraordinary amounts of vitamins A and C as well as moderate amounts of other vitamins. They are also one of the most concentrated sources of protein known. These vegetable dishes are as nutritious and healthful as they are delightfully delicious.

ABOUT THE VEGETABLES

The method of cutting the vegetable will greatly influence its final effect. Onions should ordinarily be sliced in rings. That means cutting width-wise across the onion so that the slices come apart forming little rings. The onion prepared in this way will cook better and have the best flavor for most vegetable recipes. Other vegetables should be cut in pieces large enough to retain their character, but not so large as to be too big for a bite. This means that asparagus and string beans can be in 1 to 1½-inch lengths, that spinach should be either left whole if the leaves are small, or cut once or twice, and that broccoli should be cut into bite-size florets while the stems are peeled and cut crosswise into thin slices. If any part of the broccoli stem is very woody and fibrous, it should be discarded. Zucchini cooks apart easily so should be left in larger chunks perhaps ⅛ to ½ inch thick. In some recipes, the cooking will be long enough so that the zucchini disappears. This is all right since it will form a gravy which is quite delicious and adds to the flavor of the vegetables.

Mustard Greens These are the leaves of the mustard plant, whose seeds are so widely used in flavoring and spicing foods around the world. The leafy greens grow best in a rainy, mild climate and are a spring and fall crop in temperate zones. In northern India, where the winters do not produce frost, mustard greens are grown throughout the cold months. In the very hot weather, the plants flower and produce seed and cease to put out leafy green foliage, so they are generally not available at the peak of the summer or in the hotter areas of India. In the mountains, however, they grow well and are a favorite dish, since they are extremely high in calcium, vitamins A and C and are one of the most nutritionally valuable vegetables known to man. As the leaves get older, however, they tend to become fibrous and develop a pungent, bitter quality which is more pronounced as the weather grows hotter. If the leaves are too tough they are not usable. If they are at all bitter and pungent, they must be parboiled, that is, plunged into boiling water for three to five minutes and then drained. This may have to be repeated until the strong medicinal contents of the leaves are removed. Then they become mild enough to eat. According to the ancient Ayurvedic scriptures, such greens are most digestible when all the water is removed and they are then fried in ghee, along with herbs like cumin, turmeric and coriander. (See recipe on page 64).

Spinach Spinach is another cool-weather crop which is a favorite in the mountain region, where it grows well. As a leafy green, it is not as nutritionally rich as mustard greens, but it is milder and does not ever require parboiling. Therefore, the loss that occurs in the parboiling of mustard greens does not happen with spinach. It is not necessary to cook spinach as long as mustard greens. They can be cooked together also since they complement each other nicely, one being milder and one being sharper. There is an acidic edge to spinach, however, due to the oxalic acid, but this is often neutralized by cooking it with dahl or *paneer* (see recipe on page 67).

Battwa This is known in the West as "lambs quarters" and grows throughout northern India, where it is highly prized as a green vegetable. In fact, there is probably no other leafy green (with the possible exception of dandelion) whose vitamin content can compare with it. It is also mild and delicious and is, perhaps, the most ideal of all the green vegetables. Varieties of it are used throughout the world. Battwa is prepared in much the same way as mustard and spinach and can be substituted in most of the recipes for these.

Zucchini Although zucchini is a squash that comes to us from Italy and is not used in India, it is a convenient substitute, along with yellow crookneck squash, for many of the Indian squashes which are not available in the West, such as *lauki*. Zucchini and yellow crookneck squash are especially valuable in the summer when their watery and cooling properties are helpful.

Broccoli Broccoli is another European vegetable which is little known in India, but it is a valuable substitute for Indian green vegetables, and especially for cauliflower, whose use is widespread in India but whose nutritional value is inferior.

Peppers While many varieties of peppers are available in India, they are mostly native to Mexico and have only been used in Indian cooking in the last few hundred years. The native Indian pepper is *pippali,* which is nothing even faintly resembling the *capsicum* or pepper varieties that come from Mexico. In present-day Indian cooking, the use of the pungent or hot peppers is often overdone, especially in the dishes of South India. In the mountains, this is less true. In our recipes we have often substituted a milder bell pepper or green pepper that is common in temperate zones, as it provides much of the flavor without the irritating qualities of the hot peppers.

Mushrooms Though mushrooms are not often used in the cooking of South India, in the mountains they are more widely available and frequently enjoyed. Though different varieties are used generally in the West, the commercially available mushrooms are of only one type.

Eggplant Whereas eggplant is used widely in the plains of India and in many areas because they are cheaply grown, they are generally shunned by the Brahmins of the mountains where they are considered an inferior food and thought to have untoward effects physiologically.

Potatoes Potatoes, of course, are another migrant from the West and have only entered Indian cooking in recent centuries. Though they are widely used by the poor people because they are starchy and inexpensive, they are thought by the mountain people to be best used in very limited quantities.

Tomatoes Tomatoes will ordinarily be added pureed or "stewed." The best way to prepare these is by dunking the tomatoes in boiling water for a few moments until the skins split and begin to roll back; then they can be peeled off very easily. The tomato can then be pureed in a blender or chopped with a knife or simply squeezed in the hand until it comes apart. It is always best to use fresh tomatoes even if they aren't ideal (in season and organic). However, canned tomatoes are a bit risky since the acid tomato often eats away the lead with which the can was soldered, and a dose of lead can sometimes be absorbed this way.

Basic Vegetable

Master this one and all the others will be easy.

Prepare the following:

Cut 3 medium ONIONS in ⅜ inch rings

Cut 1½ cups MUSHROOMS in ¼ inch slices

Chop 1 medium GREEN PEPPER in ½ inch squares (optional)

Cut 2 six-inch ZUCCHINI in ⅜ inch rings.

Cut 2 cups BROCCOLI, leaving florets bite-size, peeling and cutting stems very thin.

Separate broccoli stems and florets so they can be added separately.

Have on hand:

3 or 4 tablespoons of GHEE*

1 teaspoon TURMERIC

1 teaspoon WHOLE CUMIN SEED

1 teaspoon GROUND CUMIN

3 teaspoons GROUND CORIANDER

In a large, heavy, iron frypan, put ghee and heat on medium flame. Add 3 basic spices: turmeric, cumin and coriander, and fry until brown. (The spices can be fried until very dark, depending on flavor desired. Experimentation will help decide which is preferred.) Add the onions and fry until they brown and become translucent. Add mushrooms and green pepper and fry over medium-high heat so that vegetables sizzle. Then add broccoli stems and cook until they are tender. Add zucchini and broccoli florets, letting them fry 3-4 minutes after adding each.

* See page 148 for directions for making ghee.

Cook covered part of the time to bring out moisture which helps prevent sticking or burning. It is very important not to put in too many vegetables as the vegetables should be spread out so they can fry in the spices and ghee and sear. Let the water cook out so the vegetables will brown in bottom. Scrape this into the dish because it adds flavor. Add water, if necessary, and salt to taste. Cook covered for some time, and then uncovered, alternating according to whether the vegetables look as though they are getting soft. If they look as though they are beginning to cook apart, uncover; if they look as though they are tough, then cover. Sometimes the soft vegetables such as zucchini will cook apart while others retain their shape. That's all right but they shouldn't all be mushy. The length of time of cooking depends upon the kind of vegetables used. The vegetables are done when the ghee begins to ooze out forming a film on top of the vegetable. At that point, the vegetables are giving up their "heart" or essence and are ready to be served. The cook should allow enough moisture to cook out of the vegetable at this time so that it reaches the correct consistency. It can be cooked down dry enough to be served on a plate or it can be left in a soupy broth. Which is most appropriate will depend on the kind of vegetable used and the effect desired.

Variations: Other green vegetables, like spinach, green beans, or asparagus can be added. Scalded, peeled and pureed tomatoes can also be added to provide a different flavor. In a sense, many of the other recipes in this chapter are nothing more than variations of this basic recipe.

Vegetables with Celery

This is a sort of "Himalayan gumbo," a vegetable with a flavor reminiscent of the Creole cooking of New Orleans . . .

Sort and wash ¾ cup WHOLE MUNG BEANS, soak overnight. Drain, rinse thoroughly, and add 2½ cups boiling water. Cook until tender.
Meanwhile prepare the following:
    Cut 1 medium ONION into ⅜ inch rings.
    Cut 1 medium GREEN PEPPER into ½ inch rings.
    Chop 2 cups CELERY into medium pieces.
    Cut 1 eight-inch ZUCCHINI into ⅜ inch rings.
    Scald, peel and cube 1 large TOMATO.
    Chop 2½ cups (packed) fresh SPINACH.
Have on hand:
    3-4 tablespoons GHEE
    1 teaspoon TURMERIC
    1 teaspoon WHOLE CUMIN
    1 teaspoon GROUND CUMIN
    3 teaspoons GROUND CORIANDER
    1 teaspoon BLACK MUSTARD SEED

Put ghee in large, heavy iron frypan and heat on medium flame. Add first four spices and fry until seeds begin to brown. Then add mustard seed and fry until seeds begin to pop, but not explode like popcorn. Add onions and fry until they look greenish in color and are translucent. Add green pepper and let fry covering part of the time to help bring out moisture, which helps prevent sticking and burning. Fry for 3-5 minutes before adding celery.

Add vegetables in order prepared, using the same procedure. When cooked, add to cooked dahl (beans). Add 1 teaspoon of salt and simmer for 5-10 minutes. If needed, add a little more ghee before simmering. Serve with rice or whole wheat toast.

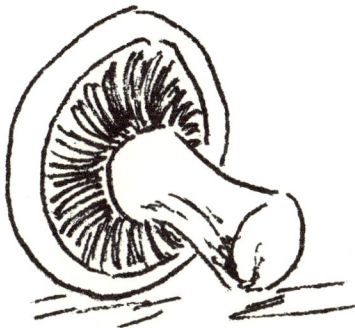

30 minutes pressure pot
45 minutes regular pot

Serves 4-6

Carrots

Carrots are a wonderful vegetable with tremendous health-giving properties. Sometimes for variety, try them this way.

Prepare the following:
  Cube 8-10 medium size CARROTS.
Have on hand:
  2 tablespoons of GHEE
  1 teaspoon MUSTARD OIL*
  2/3 teaspoon CUMIN
  1 teaspoon TURMERIC
  1 teaspoon GROUND CORIANDER
  1 teaspoon SALT

Put ghee in pressure pot and heat on medium flame. Add mustard oil and cumin. Fry a few moments. Add turmeric, ground coriander immediately. Then add dry, raw carrots. Stir a few minutes. Add salt. Cover and bring to pressure. (If using a regular pot, add ½ cup water and cover.) Cook 5 minutes under pressure (20 minutes in regular pot). Remove top. Add a little ghee if desired and cook a few moments and serve with whole wheat toast.

* While mustard oil is widely used, ghee may be substituted and is, if anything, healthier.

Kaccha-Pakka

A sort of crunchy summer treat that makes a nice snack on a hot night.

Prepare the following:
Cut 2 peeled CUCUMBERS in strips (wedges).
Have on hand:
1-1½ tablespoons GHEE
1 teaspoon TURMERIC
1 teaspoon GROUND CUMIN
½ teaspoon BLACK MUSTARD SEED

Put ghee in large, heavy, iron frypan and heat on medium flame. Add turmeric, cumin and mustard seed. Add cucumbers and saute for about 5 minutes making sure each piece fries in browned spices. Add salt to taste. Be sure not to cook too long. Cucumbers should remain crunchy. Serve with buttered whole wheat toast. Makes a delicious summer snack.

Variations:
1) Cucumbers may be thrown into boiling water 2 minutes before frying.
2) Add ¼ cup milk 2 or 3 minutes before end of cooking time.

Kashmiri Sag

From the Western Himalayas comes this mouth-watering broth with a generous complement of tender spinach.

Prepare the following:
  Clean and cut 1 large bunch fresh SPINACH.
  Thaw 1 cup frozen GREEN PEAS or use 1 cup fresh.
  Cup 1 large ONION in ⅛ inch rings.
Have on hand:
  3 tablespoons GHEE
  1 teaspoon TURMERIC
  1 teaspoon GROUND CUMIN
  2 teaspoons GROUND CORIANDER
  1 teaspoon BLACK MUSTARD SEED
  1 cup YOGURT*
  1 teaspoon SALT
  1½ cups WATER

Put ghee in pressure pot and heat on medium flame. Add turmeric, cumin and coriander and fry until brown. Add mustard seed and fry until seeds begin to pop. Add onions and fry until translucent. Then add spinach, green peas, salt and water. Cover, bring to pressure and cook for 15-20 minutes. Cool, open, add 1 cup yogurt and cook a few minutes until it thickens slightly. It's between a soup and a vegetable.

Variation: This can be made in a cast-iron frypan for a slightly different flavor and consistency.

---

* See page 149 for directions for making yogurt.

Pressure Cooker Subzi with Dahl

This is really a dahl—combined with vegetables. Almost a full meal if you add rice, and/or toast

Sort and wash 1 cup WHOLE MUNG, soak overnight, drain and rinse thoroughly.
Meanwhile, prepare the following:
    Dice 2 large POTATOES.
    Dice 2 medium ONIONS.
    Scald, peel and cube 4 medium TOMATOES.
    Clean, wash and cut 3-3½ cups GREENS. (Parboil the greens first, if they are tough or have a strong taste. Spinach or chard need not be parboiled. See p. 43 about parboiling mustard greens.)
Have on hand:
    5 cups WATER
    1½-2 teaspoons TURMERIC
    3-4 teaspoons GROUND CUMIN
    5-6 teaspoons GROUND CORIANDER
    1½ teaspoons SALT
    5-6 tablespoons GHEE

Put mung and potatoes in pressure cooker,* add 4 cups water, bring to pressure and cook 10 minutes. Open; sprinkle on turmeric, cumin and coriander. Add onions, tomatoes, greens, salt and 1 cup water. Bring to pressure again. Cook for 10-15 minutes. Be sure there is enough water to prevent sticking, but not too much because tomatoes add liquid. Open; add ghee, stir well and cook until mixture thickens and is well done. Ready to serve.

* Be aware that the hulls from whole mung beans can clog the pressure vent pipe. Pressure pot should only be filled half full with water when cooking whole mung.

Potato and Onion Subzi

A favorite for a light supper with paranthas.

Prepare the following:

    Wash 4 medium POTATOES, put in pressure cooker, cover with water, cover, bring to pressure, cook for 8 minutes.

    Cut 3 medium ONIONS in ¼ inch rings.

Have on hand:

    5 tablespoons GHEE

    1 teaspoon TURMERIC

    1 teaspoon WHOLE CUMIN

    1 teaspoon GROUND CUMIN

    3 teaspoons GROUND CORIANDER

    2 teaspoons SALT

    Put ghee in large, heavy, iron frypan and heat on medium flame. Add turmeric, cumin and coriander and fry until brown. Add onions and fry until limp but not brown. Remove potatoes from pot, peel, crush and add to the onions. Add salt, cover with hot water and cook down until almost dry. Ready to serve. Serve with Kashmiri Sag and Paranthas.

Variation: One medium tomato may be scalded, skinned, pureed and added with water to give a zip to the flavor.

Pressure Cooker Vegetable #1

It is a joy to have a recipe which is quick and delicious. The pressure cooker can be put to good use here.

Perpare the following:
   Cut 2 medium ONIONS in ¼ inch rings.
   Slice 1½ cups MUSHROOMS in ¼ inch slices.
   Cut a 6-8 inch ZUCCHINI in ⅜ inch rings.
   Chop 1½ cups BROCCOLI leaving florets whole, peeling
      and cutting stems about ⅛ inch thick.
   Scald and peel 2 medium TOMATOES and cut in ½ inch
      wedges.
Have on hand:
   5 tablespoons GHEE
   1 teaspoon TURMERIC
   1 teaspoon GROUND CUMIN
   1 teaspoon CORIANDER
   1 teaspoon GARAM MASALA*
   1½ teaspoons SALT
   2 or 3 tablespoons YOGURT

   In pressure pot put ghee and heat on medium flame. Add spices except salt and fry until brown. Add onions and fry until translucent. Then add mushrooms and fry until they begin to shrivel. Next add other vegetables and salt. Stir well and if not watery enough, add ¼ cup water. Cover, bring to pressure and cook for 10 minutes. Cool, uncover and add yogurt. Stir well and cook for 5 minutes open. Serve with rice and/or whole wheat toast, and smile. (Everyone else will!)

* A combination of spices. Can be purchased in most Indian groery stores.

Pressure Cooker Vegetable #2

Another welcome quick subzi with a slightly different twist. Try it!

Prepare the following:
    Cut 2 medium ONIONS in ⅜ inch rings.
    Scald, peel and crush 4 small or 2 large TOMATOES.
    Cut 2 cups BROCCOLI FLORETS bite-size.
    Thaw 2½ cups GREEN PEAS or shell fresh ones.
    Chop 1½ cups fresh MUSHROOMS.
    Cut 2 six-inch ZUCCHINI in ⅜ inch rings.
    Clean and chop 2 cups (packed) fresh SPINACH.
Have on hand:
    4 tablespoons GHEE
    1 teaspoon TURMERIC
    1 teaspoon GROUND CUMIN
    1 teaspoon GROUND CORIANDER
    1 teaspoon GARAM MASALA*
    2 teaspoons SALT
    2 cups boiling WATER

In pressure pot put ghee and heat on medium flame. Add spices and fry until brown. Add onions and fry until translucent. Next add tomatoes, fry a few minutes, and add broccoli, peas, mushrooms, zucchini, spinach, salt and boiling water. Cover, bring to pressure and cook 8 minutes. Turn off heat, allow to cool undisturbed until pressure goes down. The vegetable will have a watery but tasty broth. Serve with rice and/or whole wheat toast.

---

* See footnote on page 55.

Mustard/Green Peas

A delightful mustard green dish. (For a special treat add tofu.)

Prepare the following:

Clean, wash and cut 2 large bunches FRESH MUSTARD GREENS.

Have on hand:

1 large package frozen GREEN PEAS

1 teaspoon TURMERIC

2 teaspoons GROUND CUMIN

3 round teaspoons GROUND CORIANDER

1½ teaspoons SALT

3 cups WATER

¼ cup GHEE

Parboil mustard greens if necessary (see page 43). Then drain, squeeze dry, and cut. Put green peas in a strainer and run hot water over them to thaw. Put peas in pressure cooker. Then separate the mustard leaves as you put them into pressure cooker with peas. Mix well and add turmeric, cumin, coriander, salt and 3 cups water. Cover, bring to pressure and cook for 15 minutes. Cool, open and add ghee. Cook open until almost dry. Very delicious served with ground bread or whole wheat toast.

Variation: Cube about one cup of tofu (see Chapter IX) and add near the end of cooking.

Mustard Greens and Corn Meal Dodgers

The climate in the southeastern part of North America is very similar to that of the foothills of the Himalayas. In both places cornmeal and mustard green dishes are considered a delicacy. (This one comes from South Carolina.)

Have on hand:
  4 pounds tender FRESH MUSTARD GREENS
  2 cups WATER
  2 teaspoons SALT
  about ¼ cup GHEE
  2 cups CORN MEAL
  6 tablespoons FLOUR

Clean, wash and cut mustard greens. If greens are large and taste strong, it may be necessary to parboil them (see p. 43). Drain, squeeze and cut. Put in stainless steel pot, add the water and 1 teaspoon salt and cook 15-20 minutes according to quality of greens. Next, add enough ghee to season to taste and more salt if needed.

Mix corn meal, flour, 1 teaspoon salt, 2 tablespoons ghee and 1 cup hot liquid from greens. The hot liquid helps cook the meal. Mix well into a dough that can be shaped into small cakes the size of biscuits. Remove greens and bring liquid to rolling boil. Drop corn meal cakes into pot of boiling liquid. Cook until cakes look clear and meal tastes done. Greens may be put back in same pot and heated or heated in a separate saucepan. Serve while hot.

About 1 hour   Serves 3-5

Himalayan Sag

Mustard greens are a favorite in the mountains. Try them this way and you will know why.

Have on hand:
    2 large bunches of FRESH MUSTARD GREENS
    2 cups WATER
    2 tablespoons MUSTARD OIL*
    1 teaspoon TURMERIC
    1 teaspoon WHOLE CUMIN
    1 teaspoon GROUND CUMIN
    3 teaspoons GROUND CORIANDER
    1 teaspoon SALT

Clean, wash and cut mustard greens. If greens are large and taste strong it may be necessary to parboil them. (See p. 43.) Drain, squeeze into a loaf, and finely slice. Next, put mustard greens into a saucepan, add the water and let cook until tender and dry (about 30 minutes). Be sure not to let them scorch and burn.

Meanwhile, in a large, heavy, iron frypan put mustard oil (or ghee) and heat on medium flame. Add turmeric, cumin and coriander. Add salt and the sliced mustard greens. Fry for about 15 minutes, stirring to prevent sticking. Ready to serve. Serve with *paranthas.*†

* While mustard oil is widely used, ghee may be substituted and is, if anything, healthier.

† See page 131 for recipe.

Soy/Mustard

This is probably one of the most nutritious dishes ever prepared. A dynamite combination of two valuable foods.

Prepare the following:

Sort and wash 1 cup SOYBEANS. Soak overnight. Drain and rinse thoroughly. Put in pressure pot, add 3 cups water, cover, bring to pressure, cook 10-12 minutes.

Clean, wash and cut 2-2/3 cups FRESH MUSTARD GREENS. Be sure to pack cups. If greens are large and taste strong it may be necessary to parboil them. (See p. 43.) Then drain and squeeze into a loaf. Cut the loaf into very thin slices.

Chop 1-1/3 cups MUSHROOMS.

Cut 2 medium-large ONIONS into ⅜ inch rings.

Have on hand:

2 tablespoons BUTTER
3 tablespoons GHEE
1 teaspoon TURMERIC
1 teaspoon WHOLE CUMIN
1 teaspoon GROUND CUMIN
3 teaspoons GROUND CORIANDER
1¼ tablespoons BLACK MUSTARD SEED
2 cups WATER
1¼ teaspoons SALT
2 tablespoons GHEE

Into heavy, iron frypan put butter and heat on medium to medium-high flame. Add the onions and saute until they begin to brown and are translucent. Set aside to add later.

Put 3 tablespoons ghee into a large, heavy, iron frypan on medium flame. Add turmeric, cumin and coriander and fry until brown. Drain soybeans and rinse with hot water. Remove ¾ cup beans, mash and put back with others. (This will thicken and make it rich and creamy.) Add the beans, mustard greens, and chopped mushrooms to masala and fry for about 10 minutes. Add mustard seed and 2 cups water. Place all in pressure cooker, cover, bring to pressure and cook for 12 minutes. Cool, uncover, add sauteed onions, salt and 2 tablespoons ghee. Cook uncovered for 20-30 minutes. Be sure to stir to prevent sticking. Add a little water if necessary. Cook down until it's almost dry. Then serve with chapati, other roti, or whole wheat toast.

Vegetables with Soy Powder Sauce

The word soy turns some people off; maybe we should have said "Vegetables in an exquisite creamy sauce," but we wanted to remind you that this is a high protein dish.

Prepare the following:
 Cut 3 medium ONIONS in ⅜ inch rings.
 Slice 2 cups MUSHROOMS in ¼ inch slices.
 Chop 1 cup GREEN PEPPER in ½ inch squares.
 Peel and cut 1 cup BROCCOLI stems ⅛ inch thick.
 Cut 1 eight-inch ZUCCHINI into ⅜ inch rings.
 Cut 1¼-1½ cups BROCCOLI FLORETS.
Have on hand:
 5 tablespoons GHEE
 1 teaspoon TURMERIC
 1 teaspoon WHOLE CUMIN
 1 teaspoon GROUND CUMIN
 3 teaspoons GROUND CORIANDER
 1 teaspoon BLACK MUSTARD SEED
 1½ teaspoons SALT
 4 cups WATER
 ½ to ¾ cup SOY POWDER

Put ghee in a very large (14 inch) heavy, iron frypan and heat on medium flame. Add turmeric, cumin and coriander and fry until they begin to brown. Add mustard seed and fry until seeds begin to pop but not explode like popcorn. Add onions and fry until they are translucent. Then add the mushrooms and cook covered for about 3 minutes, stirring to prevent sticking. Next add the vegetables in order prepared letting each cook about 3 minutes before adding the next one. Keep covered part of the time. Do not cook too long because vegetables will be mushy. Add salt and 2 cups water; cover and cook about 10-15 minutes. Stir occasionally to prevent burning. Next add soy powder and about 1½ to 2 cups water depending upon how watery the vegetables are. Let cook at least 15 minutes or until soy powder thickens and makes a smooth, creamy sauce. It must be stirred often because powder will stick and burn. Turn off flame and cover until served (which should be as soon as possible).

Creamed Vegetable Delight

This has no cumin. It has a creamy sauce that comes from the milk that's added. If you find someone who does not rave about this, please let us know.

Prepare the following:

Cut 3 medium ONIONS in rings ¼ inch thick.

Cut 1½ cups fresh MUSHROOMS in ¼ inch slices.

Chop 1 medium GREEN PEPPER in ½ inch squares.

Cut 1 cup GREEN BEANS diagonally into 1½ inch lengths.

Cut 2 six-inch ZUCCHINI in rings ⅜ inch thick.

Chop 1 cup fresh BROCCOLI, leaving florets whole, peeling and cutting stems very thin.

Cut tips from stems of 1 cup fresh, green ASPARAGUS.

Have on hand:

2 tablespoons GHEE

¼-½ teaspoon TURMERIC

1½ teaspoons GROUND CORIANDER

⅛-¼ teaspoon BLACK MUSTARD SEED

⅛ teaspoon CAYENNE

⅛ teaspoon BLACK PEPPER

1½ teaspoons SALT

1½ to 2 cups hot WATER

1-1½ cups MILK

Put broccoli florets and asparagus tips together to be added last, and put stems and rest of tender asparagus together.

In a large, heavy, iron frypan, put ghee and heat on a medium flame. Add turmeric, coriander and mustard seed. Fry until dark brown, stirring continuously. (If mustard seed pops like popcorn, pan is too hot. They should pop but not explode.) Add onion slices and cook until they begin to look translucent. Add vegetables in order prepared, letting each fry about three minutes before adding the next. (Add broccoli bottoms after green beans.) Stir to keep from sticking or scorching on bottom. Add cayenne, black pepper and salt. Add hot water. Cover and let cook on medium heat for about 20 minutes. Stir often enough to prevent sticking. Add a cup or more of milk and let cook for 5 more minutes. This milk makes a creamy sauce, so add enough of it to make desired amount of sauce. Turn off heat and leave covered to steam until ready to serve, which shouldn't be too long. Serve with whole wheat toast.

Peas in Khoya

Rich and delicious and very high in protein. Everyone loves it.

Prepare the following:

    Chop 2 medium ONIONS very fine.

    Thaw 1 large package (1¼ pounds) frozen GREEN PEAS.

Have on hand:

- 4 tablespoons GHEE
- 1½ teaspoons TURMERIC
- ½ teaspoon GROUND CUMIN
- 1 teaspoon GROUND CORIANDER
- 3 quarts MILK (best if milk can be heating on another burner)
- 1¼ teaspoons SALT

Put ghee in large, heavy, iron frypan and heat on medium flame. Add turmeric, cumin, coriander and fry until brown. Add onions and fry until brown. Add the peas and fry briefly. Then add about a pint of milk and the salt. Let cook down on high flame and add another pint of milk. When it cooks down, if it browns on the bottom, OK. Just scrape it up and let it cook into sauce. This improves the flavor, but be sure it does not burn, because this will ruin the taste. Continue to add milk and let it cook down until the peas are tender and the milk has formed a thick sauce. Serve with rice and/or whole wheat toast.

Cashew Subzi

Rich and heavy though quite delicious. Sure to satisfy your meat-eating friends.

Prepare the following:
   Halve ½ cup of CASHEWS and soak overnight.
   Halve and slice 1 large ONION ⅜ inch thick.
   Slice thickly 1½ cups FRESH MUSHROOMS.
   Chop ½ cup GREEN PEPPER.
   Halve and·slice 2 small ZUCCHINI ⅜ inch thick.
   Scald, peel and cube 2 medium TOMATOES.
   Chop ½ cup ASPARAGUS.
Have on hand:
   2 tablespoons GHEE
   1 teaspoon TURMERIC
   1 teaspoon WHOLE CUMIN
   1 teaspoon GROUND CORIANDER
   ½ teaspoon BLACK MUSTARD SEED
   ¼ teaspoon GROUND GINGER
   1 teaspoon SALT
   ½ to 1 cup WATER

   Put ghee in wok or skillet and heat over medium flame. Add turmeric, cumin and coriander and fry until brown. Add mustard seed and ginger. Fry until it begins to look dark and smells like barbecue. Add onions and mushrooms and fry for about 3 minutes. Then add cashews and vegetables in order prepared, frying each approximately 3 minutes after each addition. Add salt and water. Cover and allow to simmer about 30 minutes, stirring occasionally to prevent sticking. Cook until liquid is minimal. Serve with rice or whole wheat toast or both.

Peas Palak Paneer

Very rich in protein, vitamins and minerals—yet not heavy at all!

Prepare the following:

    Clean, wash and cut 8 cups of FRESH SPINACH.
    Peel and cube 2 medium POTATOES.
    Cut 2 medium ONIONS into ⅜ inch rings.
    Cut 1 large GREEN PEPPER into ½ inch squares.
    Thaw 1¼ pound package of frozen GREEN PEAS.
    Make PANEER* using 1 gallon of MILK and cube.

Have on hand:

    4 tablespoons GHEE
    1 teaspoon TURMERIC
    1 teaspoon CUMIN SEED
    1 teaspoon GROUND CUMIN
    3 teaspoons GROUND CORIANDER
    1 teaspoon BLACK MUSTARD SEED
    1½ teaspoons SALT
    4 cups WATER
    ⅛ teaspoon GROUND RED PEPPER

    Put ghee in large wok and heat on medium flame. Add first four spices until they begin to brown. Add mustard seed and fry until the seeds begin to pop. (They should pop but not explode.) Then add onions and fry until brown. Add green pepper and fry for about 3 or 4 minutes. Add rest of vegetables and water. Cover and cook about 1 hour. Check often to see that the water does not cook out. Add paneer, red pepper and hot water if needed. Cook, uncovered for 30-45 minutes, stirring often because paneer will cause it to stick and burn. Serve with whole wheat toast.

---

* See page 150 for directions for making paneer.

Stuffed Peppers

If you're a pepper lover, you're sure to like this.

Prepare the following:

Sort and grind ¾ cup (dry) split washed MUNG DAHL.
Finely chop 1 large ONION.
Finely dice 1 large POTATO.
Chop into ¼ inch pieces 1 eight-inch ZUCCHINI.
Chop very small 1½ cups BROCCOLI (stems and florets).
Measure ¼ cup RAISINS.
Cut tops just deep enough to clean out seed and pulp of 6 medium GREEN PEPPERS.

Have on hand:

4 tablespoons GHEE
1 teaspoon TURMERIC
1 teaspoon WHOLE CUMIN
1 teaspoon GROUND CUMIN
3 teaspoons GROUND CORIANDER
1 teaspoon BLACK MUSTARD SEED
1½ teaspoons SALT

Put ghee in a large, heavy, iron frypan and heat on medium flame. Add first four spices and fry until brown. Add mustard seed and fry until it begins to pop. Add mung and onions stirring constantly and slowly add hot water. Next, add potatoes, zucchini, broccoli, raisins and salt. Cook about 40 minutes or until thickened and vegetables are soft. Be sure to stir often and add water to prevent sticking or burning. Stuff peppers with this mixture and cook in medium oven (350°) about 25-30 minutes. Stuffs 6 medium green peppers. Serve while hot.

Mustard Greens and Paneer

Sweet, rich and meaty, proving that leafy green vegetables can be delicious.

Prepare the following:
>   Make PANEER* using 2 quarts MILK and the juice of 2
>   LEMONS.
>   Clean, wash and chop 2 large bunches of fresh MUSTARD
>   GREENS.
>   Cut 2 medium ONIONS into rings ¼ inch thick.
>   Chop 1 medium-large GREEN PEPPER into ½ inch pieces.

Have on hand:
>   5 tablespoons GHEE
>   1 teaspoon TURMERIC
>   1 teaspoon GROUND CUMIN
>   3 teaspoons GROUND CORIANDER
>   3 teaspoons BLACK MUSTARD SEED
>   1 teaspoon SALT

If greens are large and taste strong it may be necessary to parboil them. (See p. 43.) Drain and squeeze into a loaf. Cut loaf into very thin slices and put in a saucepan. Add cubed paneer and water and cook. Be sure to stir often enough to prevent sticking. Put 3 tablespoons of ghee into a large, heavy frypan and heat on medium flame. Add turmeric, cumin and coriander and 1 teaspoon mustard seed and fry slowly until seeds begin to pop. (The seeds should not explode.) Add half of the onions and fry

---

* For details see recipe on page 150.

until translucent. Then add green pepper and fry until brown. Add this and salt to greens and paneer. Continue to cook. Add a little water along the way as needed but only a little at a time. Now fry remainder of the onions in 2 tablespoons ghee until onions are clear. Remove onions and put aside to use in another dish. Then add 2 teaspoons mustard seeds and fry until crisp. Put into saucepan with greens and continue to cook until almost dry. Should cook about an hour altogether.

VI
Rice

VI Rice

Rice has been traced to its origins in India about 3,000 B.C. Within a couple hundred years, it was a staple in both India and China. The number of varieties that have evolved since then are countless. Each has its own particular flavor, is suited to its own particular climate and has different nutritional properties. In recent times, however, new varieties of rice have been developed not so much for their nutritional qualities or their flavor, but more for their yield and their response to artificial fertilizers. This has changed the quality of much rice and flooded the market with a low-grade, rather unpleasant grain that is hardly tempting.

There is also a furor over brown rice, as though the color of rice could determine its nutritional value. Actually, what is important is not that the rice be *brown* but that the rice be milled little or not at all. Milling is the process that removes the bran or outer coating of the rice grain. Actually rice, like other grains, has two coats. The first is a husk which flakes off easily, using the fingernails. Then there is a tightly adhering coat which is like the bran of wheat and gives the rice its characteristic color. This cannot be removed easily, and when it is removed, an elaborate process of "milling" is necessary. The result is a rice that is "polished." Technically the process is called *pearling*, and though it is not common to speak of "pearled rice," actually "polished rice" goes through the same process that barley does when it is "pearled." After the pearling which removes the bran, rice may further be polished to give it an attractive sheen. During the various milling processes, rice will lose approximately 10% of its protein, 85% of the fat, and 70% of the minerals as well as a large part of the B vitamins which it contained. Such losses are much reduced when the rice is steamed or parboiled before milling, as is the custom in India.*

But all unmilled rice is not brown. The color of the rice before it is milled depends on the natural color of its coating or bran. When the outer husk is removed, the inner coating or bran of each variety will be found to have a characteristic color. Most of those commonly grown commercially are brown. Others are red and some are simply white or cream-colored.

The red rice is one of the oldest varieties and is at home in the foothills of the Himalayan Mountains. It was grown for thousands of years there and still is, by farmers who treasure it for its nutritiousness and its unique flavor. The ancient writings on Indian medicine recommend it highly. Yet it is seldom available commercially these days because its yield is not high and it is not profitable to grow.

In most of our recipes, we use basmati rice, a high grade, fragrant and fine quality rice which is naturally white without milling. It is grown in one of the valleys nestled in the foothills of the Himalayas and has been treasured centuries for its delicate aroma. When this rice is cooking, the fragrance can be noticed throughout the house, quite a contrast to the rather unpleasant odor that comes from commercially grown rice, be it milled or brown. Those interested in nutrition sometimes wonder why they are unable to convince people to eat "brown rice." They ignore completely the fact that the variety of rice may not be particularly good and may have an objectionable taste. Simply leaving on the bran does not make a poor rice good, though it does make it somewhat better nutritionally. Unfortunately, it may at the same time, make an objectionable taste even stronger especially if the rice is not fresh, since some unpolished rice can

* For further details on the pros and cons of milling and parboiling see *Diet and Nutrition* by Rudolph Ballentine, M.D., published by the Himalayan Institute.

become rancid, and for this reason many people have learned to balk at eating "brown rice."

A meatless diet of domesticated foods (those grown agriculturally) will almost always lean heavily on some combination of grain (rice or wheat, for example) and legumes (such as beans, peas, lentils, etc.). The common diet of those populations around the world where health is best is usually found to be based on some such combination. In China, it is rice and soybeans; in Mexico, it's corn and red beans (*tortillas* and *frijoles*); in most parts of India, and especially around the mountains, it is rice or wheat and dahl (i.e., legumes such as mung beans). As a staple grain in the diet, rice is one of the best. It contains no gluten as do wheat, oats, rye and barley, and therefore does not cause many of the problems that those grains can. It has been used with great benefit in patients who have high blood pressure and is revered throughout Asia as a sacred food. In most parts of America, unfortunately, rice is neglected—possibly because the varieties available are not tasty or nutritious; or possibly because most people do not know how to prepare it properly.

The preparation of rice is both simple and delicate. A cook who understands rice will simply throw it in a pot with some water, set it on the stove, come back in a little while, lift the lid, and show you a full pot of fluffy, tender and delicious rice. A cook who does not understand rice will labor endlessly with it and still turn out a soggy, gummy, repulsive mess.

Actually, the less that is done to rice, the better it is. It should be picked over to make sure it contains no tiny pebbles, no dirt, and no spoiled grains that would give it a bad flavor. Then it should be rinsed in cool water until the water is clear. Then the proper amount of water is added, the rice is brought to a boil, covered, turned down to low heat, and allowed to cook until it absorbs all the water. Then it is perfect. (For details, see recipe in this section.)

The amount of water that is put in the rice is of course the crucial issue. But if too much is put in, not all is lost. The rice can still be salvaged by putting a cloth over the pot and then pushing the lid down over it. If it cooks on low heat this way for some time, much of the water will rise as steam, condense in the cloth, and can be simply removed. If too little water was put in, a small amount of boiling water can be gently poured into the pot, taking care not to disturb the rice.

Probably the most important thing in cooking rice is not to stir it. Rice must breathe. As it cooks, it forms natural channels or tunnels that run through the network of grains. These little passageways are what allow the steam to escape and the rice to cook properly and evenly. If this network is disturbed through stirring, the rice will lose its fluffy quality, and the individual grains will become gummy and stick together.

The rice can be cooked either with a bit more water which makes it very fluffy, light and easy to digest or can be cooked with less water in which case it will be a bit tougher and chewier but more demanding for the stomach. For those who are very sick or debilitated, rice can be boiled in a great deal of water, and the water strained away. This rice is less nutritious but easier to digest. The liquid which is strained off, however, contains many vitamins and minerals, and it is often used as a medicine or replacement for those who have lost fluid through diarrhea or vomiting.

Leftover rice can be used within a day or two if it is kept refrigerated. In this case, it should be dumped in a hot steel pot with a little ghee in the bottom. The rice is then fried in the ghee stirring constantly until it is coated well and sizzling. Then it can be covered for a few moments so that it regains its tenderness.

Many dishes are made with rice as a base. We include in this section those which are best suited to accompany dahl and vegetables. Sweet dishes are sometimes also made of rice, the most famous of which is *kheer*. (See section on sweet dishes.) Though it contains a little bit of sugar, it is still considered *sattvic* or a wholesome dish and is definitely a delight. Like most sweet dishes in India, however, it is usually reserved for special occasions.

Plain Rice

This is the basic recipe. Indian rice, which is parboiled and lightly milled, will cook quickly. Brown rice will take longer.

Clean the number of cups of rice needed. Wash in cool water until water is clear. Put into saucepan large enough for rice to swell. Add 2 cups of water for each cup of rice. Bring to boil, cover, turn to lowest possible heat and cook. Do not stir. Listen to it boil occasionally. When it begins to sizzle as if water has boiled out or when top grains "stand at attention," turn off heat. Leave covered for at least 5 minutes. Then serve.

"Brown Rice"

Actually, this is white rice—colored by brown(ed) onions!

Prepare the following:
    Clean and wash 1 cup BASMATI RICE. Drain.
    Chop 1 large ONION into half-inch pieces.
Have on hand:
    3 tablespoons GHEE
    1 teaspoon SALT
    2 cups WATER

    Put ghee in stainless steel pot and heat on medium flame. Add onion, lower flame and fry slowly until very dark brown. Add washed rice and fry for a few minutes mixing well. Then add 1 teaspoon salt and 2 cups water. Bring to a rolling boil. Cover, lower heat to lowest flame and cook until you hear it begin to fry on bottom and grains "stand at attention." Serve immediately.

Variation: After onions are fried until translucent, add 1 cup finely chopped mushrooms, cook until tender, and proceed as above.

Picku's Rice

Another delightful way to prepare rice.

Prepare the following:
    Cut 1 large ONION into ¼ inch slices.
    Quarter 1 cup MUSHROOMS.
    Clean and wash 1½ cups BASMATI RICE.
Have on hand:
    2 tablespoons GHEE
    1½ teaspoons WHOLE CUMIN
    1½ teaspoons SALT
    3 cups plus 2 tablespoons WATER

Put ghee in a large saucepan and heat on medium flame. Add onions and fry until brown. Add mushrooms, cumin, salt, about 2 tablespoons water; cover and cook for 10 minutes. Add rice, 3 cups water and mix well. Cook on lowest heat until rice grains "stand at attention."

Khichari

A mild delight, pleasant to even the most delicate stomach and yet rich and nourishing. With a combination of grain and legume, it forms a perfect protein.

Prepare the following:
    Clean and wash ½ cup BASMATI RICE.
    Clean and wash ½ cup split MUNG DAHL.
    Chop ½ inch fresh GINGER ROOT very fine (or grate).
Have on hand:
    2 tablespoons GHEE
    1 teaspoon TURMERIC
    1 teaspoon GROUND CUMIN
    1 teaspoon GROUND CORIANDER
    1½ teaspoons SALT
    about 3 cups WATER

Put ghee in pressure pot and heat on medium flame. Add turmeric, cumin, coriander, and ginger root and fry until slightly brown. Then add dahl and rice and fry for several minutes. Next add salt and water, cover, bring to pressure and cook 3-5 minutes. Open, stir and serve.

Variation: If spices are halved and washed split mung is used, this dish is very good for those whose digestion is disordered.

Pullao

A favorite Indian trick is adding vegetables to rice before it cooks so that the flavors mingle.

Prepare the following:
    Mince (very fine) 1 medium ONION.
    Quarter 1 cup small MUSHROOMS.
    Dice (very fine) 1 cup CARROTS.
    Thaw about 1 cup frozen GREEN PEAS.
    Clean and wash 1½ cups BASMATI RICE.
Have on hand:
    4 tablespoons GHEE
    1 teaspoon TURMERIC
    1 teaspoon WHOLE CUMIN
    1 teaspoon GROUND CUMIN
    3 teaspoons GROUND CORIANDER
    1 teaspoon BLACK MUSTARD SEED
    1½ teaspoons SALT
    2¾ cups HOT WATER

Put ghee in a large, heavy, iron pan and heat on medium flame. Add turmeric, cumin and coriander and fry until seeds begin to brown. Then add mustard seed and fry slowly until they begin to pop. Add onions and fry until they have a yellowish color. Add mushrooms and fry for 2-3 minutes. Then add carrots and peas. Fry until almost done (about 10-15 minutes). Add rice, salt and water. Stir well until vegetables and rice are evenly distributed. Let come to a boil, reduce to lowest heat and cover. Cook until a hissing sound is produced as mixture begins to fry on bottom and the grains begin to "stand at attention." Turn off heat and let steam for about 10 minutes. Serve.

Nine Jewels

NAURATNI or SARSO ALOO PULLAO

A sort of mountain paella. Sweet, mild and delicious.

Prepare the following:

Sort, wash and soak 1-1½ cups SOY BEANS overnight at room temperature. Drain, rinse and put in pressure pot.

Add 3 cups WATER, cover, bring to pressure and cook for 15 minutes. Drain and rinse with hot water. (As an alternative, ¾ cup of kidney beans and ¾ cup of whole green mung beans may be used. They should be cooked under pressure for 10 minutes.)*

Meanwhile:

Cut 3 small ONIONS in ⅜ inch rings.

Thaw 1 large package (1 pound) frozen GREEN PEAS.

Slice 2 medium, peeled POTATOES in ⅜ inch slices.

Clean and wash thoroughly 1 cup BASMATI RICE.

Cut 1 medium GREEN PEPPER into ½ inch squares.

Quarter ½ cup MUSHROOMS.

Clean and chop 2 cups (packed) MUSTARD GREENS and parboil. (See p. 43.) Drain and squeeze into a loaf. Slice in thin slices.

Have on hand:

4 tablespoons GHEE

1 teaspoon TURMERIC

1 teaspoon WHOLE CUMIN

---

* If mung beans are used in the pressure pot be aware that their hulls can clog the pressure vent pipe. Remember not to fill pressure pot over half full of water when cooking whole mung.

3 teaspoons GROUND CORIANDER
1½ teaspoons SALT
2½ cups BOILING WATER

Put ghee in 10-inch-wide deep pot and heat on medium flame. Add turmeric, cumin and coriander and fry until brown. Then add onions and fry until brown. Add green pepper and fry for about 3 minutes. Then add and mix peas, potatoes, mushrooms, rice, mustard greens, cooked beans, salt and boiling water. Mix thoroughly until rice and vegetables are evenly distributed. Cover and cook undisturbed over lowest heat until rice and potatoes are done—about 20 or 25 minutes.

The rice will soak up all the moisture and cook to a good texture, creating a fine network in the vegetable. It should not be stirred after all ingredients are added and the heat should be very low or it will burn. Serve with whole wheat toast.

Fakir Ki Khichari

A Fakir is a wandering monk. This is a whole meal—dahl, rice and vegetable—that can be cooked very simply in a single pot over a fire in a short time, before moving on . . .

Prepare the following:

Sort and wash ¾ cup WHOLE MUNG BEANS,* soak overnight. Drain and rinse thouroughly. Put in pressure pot, add 1 inch water (about 2½ cups), bring to pressure and cook about 10 minutes.

Sort ¾ cup BASMATI RICE, wash until water is clear and soak in hot water.

Slice 2 small ONIONS into ⅜ inch rings.

Cut 1 medium GREEN PEPPER into ½ inch pieces.

Slice ½-¾ cup MUSHROOMS into ¼ inch slices.

Cut 1¼ cups BROCCOLI (florets whole and stems thin).

Clean and cut 1-1½ cup FRESH SPINACH.

Have on hand:

5 tablespoons GHEE

1 teaspoon TURMERIC

1 teaspoon GROUND CUMIN

2½-3 teaspoons GROUND CORIANDER

2 cups WATER

1 teaspoon SALT

⅛ teaspoon RED PEPPER

Put 3 tablespoons ghee into large, heavy iron frypan and heat on medium flame. Add turmeric, cumin, coriander and fry until brown. Add onions and green pepper and fry for 2 or 3

---

* See footnote page 84.

minutes. Then add mushrooms and drained rice and fry briefly. Add broccoli and spinach. Stir well. Put all, including beans, in pot and add about 2 cups water (enough to cover), salt, red pepper, and 2 tablespoons ghee. (NOTE: do not be generous with the red pepper until you know how hot you like it.) Mix well, cover and cook for 10-15 minutes until stiff and the rice and dahl are cooked to required tenderness. Heat must be low and care must be taken to prevent sticking and burning. The rice takes up lots of moisture and dahl has a tendency to stick. When mixture is stiff and the rice is tender, it's ready to serve.

Green Rice

Rich and delicious. A perfect hot supper served with toast.

Prepare the following:

Cut 3 small to medium ONIONS in ⅜ inch rings.

Quarter 2 cups medium-sized MUSHROOMS.

Clean and wash 2 cups BASMATI RICE in hot water.

Cut florets from medium-sized spear of BROCCOLI; peel stem and cut into very thin slices.

Cut 1 large GREEN PEPPER into cubes.

Cut 2 six-inch ZUCCHINI into ⅜ inch slices.

Wash and cut 2 bunches of fresh SPINACH.

Have on hand:

3 tablespoons GHEE

1½ teaspoons TURMERIC

3 teaspoons GROUND CUMIN

4½ teaspoons GROUND CORIANDER

1½ cups GHEE SKIMMINGS (top part removed while making ghee)* or butter

1½-2 quarts MILK

about ½ teaspoon SALT

In a large, 14-inch frying pan, place ghee, turmeric, cumin and coriander. Fry until a dark brown, then add onions and saute. Add mushrooms and saute some more, adding the ghee skimmings. Add rice, fry it a bit, then add broccoli, green pepper, zucchini and spinach. At this point, it may be necessary to add

* For details, see recipe on page 148.

milk. (Don't add water.) When the mixture begins to cook down, thicken and stick too much, more milk should be added (probably about 1½ to 2 quarts altogether will be necessary). Add salt, cover and allow to cook. It will have to be stirred frequently to prevent sticking. It should be cooked down until it is very thick and can be served on a plate. It will have to cook for about 30 minutes, maybe as much as 45 minutes. At the end the broccoli should be a little bit tough, not completely soft, but the zucchini should be beginning to cook apart. This is creamy and scrumptious. The milk and leafy greens give it a high protein content.

Picku's Pullao

Almost a meal in itself. This is a very special way to prepare rice.

Prepare the following:
    Mince (very fine) 1 medium ONION.
    Quarter 1 cup MUSHROOMS.
    Dice (very fine) 1 cup CARROTS.
    Thaw about 1 cup GREEN PEAS or use fresh ones.
    Clean and wash 1½ cups BASMATI RICE.
Have on hand:
    4 tablespoons GHEE
    1½ teaspoons WHOLE CUMIN
    1½ teaspoons SALT
    2¾ cups WATER

In a large, heavy, iron frypan heat ghee on medium-high flame. Add the onions and fry until brown. Next add mushrooms and cook for about 5 minutes. Add peas, carrots, cumin and salt, and fry until almost done. Add uncooked rice, water, and mix well until evenly distributed. Put in a large saucepan, cover and cook at lowest heat until it begins to fry at bottom and the grains of rice "stand at attention." Turn off heat and leave covered until ready to serve.

VII

Dahls

VII Dahls

Dahl is an Indian catch-all term which is used for beans, peas, lentils and so forth. Because such legumes as beans, peas, and lentils are a very important complement to grains, the average Indian meal always contains a dish of dahl. It seems to be understood in India as well as in most parts of the world that grains and legumes, when combined, form a complete food. It has been said that their proteins are complementary, combining to form a complete protein (one in which all the essential amino acids are present in the proper proportions for man to use).* Dried beans and peas have been found by Western researchers to build up the hemoglobin content of the blood much better than any other food.

Each country seems to have its favorite legume, depending on its climatic conditions, its traditions and its history. In China, Japan and Southeast Asia, for example, the soybean is king. Soybeans have also been used in India and probably were known there in ancient times, but there are also many other different varieties of beans and peas that are prominent in Indian cooking. The most prominent among them are chick peas, mung beans, fresh peas, and to a lesser extent: *urad, arahar, massor* and *rajma* (kidney beans).

Chana (and chick peas) What we call chick peas in America or *garbanzos* in Spain are a staple in the Middle East

---

* See *Diet & Nutrition* by Rudolph Ballentine, M.D. for a detailed explanation of this point.

whence they apparently spread through the Mediterranean countries into the Iberian peninsula. Their use also extends East into Afghanistan with which they are identified in India, where they are called *kabuli chana*. A smaller but similar legume, which looks like a darkened and shriveled garbanzo is called in India *chana*. "Chana" means "pebble" and when dry, before cooking, they are very hard and odd-shaped like a bowl of brown pebbles. What's more, the peas have a heavy, tough skin that prevents easy cooking of them so even when ready to eat they retain a nearly crunchy consistency. The Punjabis love to sprout them and eat them raw. Partial sprouting (24-48 hours at room temperature) makes them easier to cook and digest.

More often chana is split and has the husk-like skin removed. This makes it vastly easier to cook and in this form *chana dal,* as it is called, is the most commonly used legume in the Indian subcontinent. Chana is even ground into a flour, called *besan* or "gram flour" which with yogurt is the basis of *karhi* (curry) and which is sometimes mixed with wheat flour to make a high-protein (grain/legume) *chapati.*

Like other dahls, chana is especially appreciated when picked fresh, before it completely matures and dries, and is cooked much like garden peas.

Mung Beans *(moong dahl)* Though chick peas may be the legume consumed in the largest quantity in India, mung beans are easily the most highly regarded. A tiny green legume which has become famous in this country as a source of sprouts (mung bean sprouts) for use in Chinese cooking, mung beans actually originated in India, where they are usually cooked as a bean rather than sprouted. Mung beans are said to be the lightest to digest, the most nourishing and healthy of all the legumes. They are especially recommended for those who are engaged in spiritual practices and need to maintain a lightness, alertness and clarity of mind. They are available in a wide variety of forms. Most often they are used split, in which case they may either be "washed," (meaning that the husks have been removed so they are pure white), or they may be split and the husk left on (in which case the rounded side is still green). Both are delicious though the flavor is different in each case. The washed ones are used for a more delicate taste and also in sweet dishes. Mung beans or *mung dahl* are also available in their whole, unsplit form, in which case they make a hearty, meaty sort of stew. They require much more cooking in this case—hours, in fact. This may be part of the reason for the popularity of split mung beans.

Urad dahl (black gram) First cousin of the mung bean is *urad dahl,* which is of the same shape and size approximately, but black rather than green. Though they look very much alike and are botanically related, their properties and taste are really quite different. While mung beans are light and easy to digest, urad dahl is heavy and almost greasy in texture. It produces a very rich dish almost reminiscent of pork. It is said to be extremely nourishing, capable of building up the body, increasing weight, and replenishing tissue. Because of its heaviness, however, many people find it difficult to handle. Nevertheless, different varieties of urad are available, and the tiny variety grown in the Himalayan Mountains is much lighter, tastier, and easier to digest. It has most of the virtues of the other urad without its disadvantages. Unfortunately, such tiny urad is often difficult to find.

Peas *(muttar)* Fresh green garden peas common in the West are also highly regarded in India. Suited to the cool climate of the mountains, they are particularly popular around the foothills of the Himalayas, though they are used widely in many parts of India. Because they are green and also have a high protein content, they supply an ideal combination of vitamins, protein and carbohydrate. They are the basis for many delicious dishes such as "Peas Paneer."

Other Dahls Another dahl of particular value is *arahar* which is prized because of its tendency to warm the body and produce heat. For this reason it is particularly used in winter in parts of India like the mountains where the weather becomes chilly but heating facilities are minimal. *Masoor* is another dahl that looks from the outside very much like lentils, but when husked, turns out to have a pinkish-colored interior. Another dahl that is favored in Punjab, south and west of the mountains, is called *rajma,* known to us as "kidney beans." Unfortunately, they are rather heavy and best left, perhaps, to the vigorous digestion of a Sikh warrior. Many other varieties of dahl are used, like *lobia, moth,* and so forth.

When serving dahl, it is important to remember that only a small amount is necessary to balance the meal. The amount of legume in proportion to the grain may be smaller. If excessive amounts of dahl are served, the meal will become heavy and burdensome. In India, it is customary to serve dahl in individual little bowls, and it functions much as a gravy or sauce. It is cooked with a lot of water and has a soupy sort of consistency. It can then be spooned over rice, or bread may be dipped into it.

All dahls (beans and peas) should be sorted for stones, washed, soaked overnight, drained, and rinsed thoroughly before cooking whenever possible. It is also important to remember that dahl must be well cooked if it is to be well digested. The best test is to pick up one of the beans and squeeze it between the fingers. If it can be completely mashed without a great deal of difficulty, then it is done. Otherwise, it probably needs more cooking.

In Indian cooking, dahl is almost always seasoned with the basic spices. In the mountains, those favored are turmeric, cumin, and coriander, though often mustard seed and/or ginger are added. A tiny dash of cayenne is also nice, as it increases digestive fire and, along with the other spices, helps to reduce the tendency of the dahl to form gas.

A well-seasoned, properly cooked dahl served in the right proportion to the rest of the meal is practically a necessity. It is the source of the best protein and if one's diet contains no meat, then one serving of dahl, peas, or beans of some sort should be included every day. For those who have been accustomed to a high protein or meat-containing diet and want something that they can get their teeth into and that will "stick to their ribs," dahl can be prepared as a hearty, semi-solid stew. This will satisfy even the most ravenous appetite and is fit food for a northern lumberjack. (See the recipes for "Chocolate" Dahl and for Chick Pea Stew, both of which are hearty and "meaty.")

Quick Mung Dahl

This is the quickest way to cook whole dahl. Split mung dahl can be done in the same way and requires much less time still.

The first order of business is always sorting the dahl, which means throwing out those which look discolored or misshapen and, more importantly, removing all the rocks, the tiny pebbles or stones which might have been included with the dahl. (Otherwise they will ruin your teeth!)

Prepare the following:
Sort and wash 2 cups WHOLE MUNG DAHL, soak overnight, drain and rinse thoroughly. Put into a pressure pot and cover with about 3 inches of lukewarm water. Put on heat, bring to pressure, let it cook for about 10-15 minutes;* turn it off and let cool by itself without opening.

Have on hand:
3 tablespoons GHEE
1 teaspoon TURMERIC
2 teaspoons CUMIN
3 teaspoons GROUND CORIANDER
1-1½ teaspoons SALT

Meanwhile, in a frying pan put ghee, add spices and fry until brown. When the pressure is down, open the pressure pot and dump spices in. Put a little bit of dahl into the frying pan, stir it around and then put this back. Add a little more ghee and salt. Turn up the heat, cook it open for another 5-10 minutes. It is ready to eat. It should be quite soupy.

---

* Watch the pot to make sure the vent doesn't become clogged. A six-quart pot is best.

Basic Whole Mung

The simplest (one pot) way to turn out hearty whole mung.

Prepare the following:
  Sort and wash 1 cup WHOLE MUNG DAHL. Soak
  overnight. Drain and rinse thoroughly.
  Slice 1 large ONION in ⅜ inch slices.
Have on hand:
  3 tablespoons GHEE
  1 teaspoon TURMERIC
  1½ teaspoons WHOLE CUMIN SEED
  2 teaspoons GROUND CORIANDER
  1 teaspoon SALT
  WATER

  Put mung in a large stainless saucepan, add water to cover 2
inches over the dahl. Cook on medium high heat until broth
thickens somewhat but dahl remains intact yet soft enough to be
mashed (approximately 15 to 20 minutes). It may be necessary to
add more boiling water.* When dahl is nearly done, put ghee in a
cast iron frypan on medium flame. Add spices and fry until
brown. Add onions and fry until translucent. Then pour some
cooked dahl into hot spices and onion, stir well and pour mixture
back into saucepan with remaining dahl. Add salt to taste. Cook
for a few more minutes. When ghee begins to come out it's ready
to serve. Serve with rice.

---

* If water is needed at anytime during the cooking process of dahl, it should be brought to a rolling
boil and then added. This will keep the beans and water from separating.

Whole Mung

This is really a vegetable recipe that contains dahl. A convenient way, however, to sneak in the protein for those who think they don't like beans, peas, etc.

Prepare the following:
    Sort and wash 1 cup WHOLE MUNG DAHL, soak overnight. Drain and rinse thoroughly.
Meanwhile:
    Chop 1 large ONION into small pieces.
    Chop finely ½ large GREEN PEPPER.
    Slice 1 cup MUSHROOMS into ⅜ inch slices.
    Scald, peel and mash 1 large TOMATO.
Have on hand:
    3 tablespoons GHEE
    1 teaspoon TURMERIC
    1 teaspoon WHOLE CUMIN
    1 teaspoon GROUND CUMIN
    3 teaspoons GROUND CORIANDER
    1 teaspoon BLACK MUSTARD SEED
    1 teaspoon SALT

Put whole mung dahl in large saucepan and cover with water about 2 inches over the dahl. Cook on medium high heat until broth thickens somewhat but dahl remains intact yet soft enough to be mashed. Add boiling water if necessary.

When dahl is nearly cooked, put ghee into large, heavy frypan and heat on medium flame. Add turmeric, cumins and coriander and fry until brown. Add black mustard seed and fry until seeds begin to pop. Add onion and fry until translucent. Then add green pepper and mushrooms. Fry on slow heat until onions are very dark. Add tomato and fry briefly. Pour some cooked dahl into hot spices and vegetable mixture. Stir well and pour everything back into saucepan containing dahl. Add salt and cook for a few more minutes. When ghee starts to come out it's ready to serve. Serve with rice.

Washed Split Mung

A simple, basic recipe—tastes good day after day after day!

Prepare the following:
   Slice 1 medium ONION into ¾ inch slices.
   Slice 1 cup MUSHROOMS into ¼ inch slices (optional).
Have on hand:
   1 cup WASHED SPLIT MUNG DAHL (Sort it, wash it,
      soak several hours—approximately 3 to 4. Drain and rinse
      thoroughly.)
   4 cups WATER
   3 tablespoons GHEE
   1 teaspoon TURMERIC
   1 teaspoon WHOLE CUMIN
   1 teaspoon GROUND CUMIN
   3 teaspoons GROUND CORIANDER
   1 teaspoon BLACK MUSTARD SEED
   1 teaspoon SALT

   Put dahl in a stainless steel saucepan, add water and cook
on medium high heat until broth thickens somewhat but dahl
remains intact yet soft enough to be mashed. (About 10
minutes.) Meanwhile, put ghee in a large, heavy frypan and heat
on medium flame. Add turmeric, cumin, and coriander, and fry
until cumin seed begins to brown. Add black mustard seed and
continue to fry until seeds begin to pop, not explode like
popcorn. Add onions and mushrooms and fry briefly. Pour some
of the cooked dahl into hot spices, onions, etc. Put all back into
the saucepan, add salt to taste and stir well. Cover and cook until
onions and mushrooms are tender. Add boiling water as needed.

When ghee begins to come out, it is ready to serve. (Do not overcook.)

Variations:

1) Washed split *tuar (arahar)* or washed split chana (dark chick peas) may be used instead of washed split mung.

2) Boil 2 eggs in dahl while cooking. Remove eggs, shell and chop them, then add to dahl.

3) Split unwashed mung (with husks) may be used.

"Doves" Smothered in Gravy

Of course, it is not really doves and maybe you have never eaten doves anyhow, but for those who have, the taste might be familiar. It's rich and hearty and good in the wintertime. Served with rice and/or toast, this is a full meal.

Prepare the following:
  Cut 3 medium-large ONIONS in ⅜ inch rings.
  Slice 2 cups MUSHROOMS about ¼ inch thick.
  Cut 1½ cups BROCCOLI florets and 1½ cups broccoli stems (thin).
  Sort and wash 1 cup WASHED SPLIT MUNG DAHL. Soak for several hours (approximately 3 to 4), drain and rinse thoroughly. Cook in water (approximately 2 inches over the beans) until tender.
Have on hand:
  4 tablespoons GHEE
  1 teaspoon TURMERIC
  1 teaspoon WHOLE CUMIN
  1 teaspoon GROUND CUMIN
  1 teaspoon BLACK MUSTARD SEED
  1½ teaspoons SALT

Meanwhile, put ghee in a large, heavy frypan and heat on medium flame. Add turmeric, whole cumin and ground cumin and fry until seeds are light brown. Then add slowly black mustard seed and fry until seeds begin to pop but they should not explode like popcorn. If they do, lower the heat. Add the onions and fry until they are limp and begin to change color. Then add mushrooms and fry for 2-3 minutes. If they begin to stick and burn, add just enough water to prevent this. Next add broccoli and cook for 2-3 minutes. Add cooked mung and salt. Let simmer for 20-30 minutes, adding water if necessary. Stir often to keep from sticking and burning. Cook down until vegetables are in a brown gravy. Serve with rice and/or whole wheat toast.

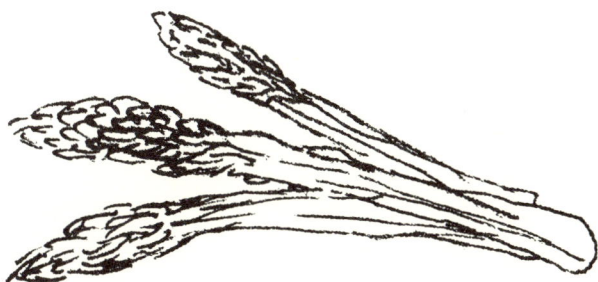

Karhi

This is a very nourishing dish containing a sort of chick pea flour, yogurt, and green peas, all of which are high in protein. It's a favorite that deserves frequent preparation.

Prepare the following:

Cut 2 large ONIONS into ⅜ inch rings.

Thaw 1 large package of frozen GREEN PEAS.

Cut 2 cups BROCCOLI leaving florets bite-size, peeling and cutting stems very thin.

Have on hand:

5 tablespoons GHEE

1 teaspoon TURMERIC

1 teaspoon GROUND CUMIN

1 teaspoon GROUND CORIANDER

½ teaspoon FENUGREEK

1 teaspoon BLACK MUSTARD SEED

¾ cup BESAN (gram flour)

1 pint YOGURT*

2 teaspoons SALT

2 cups WATER

Put ghee in a large, heavy frypan and heat on medium flame.

Add turmeric, cumin and coriander, and then add the fenugreek and fry until brown. Add black mustard seed and fry until the seeds begin to pop. Add onions and fry until brown. Add peas and broccoli. Next add besan, yogurt, salt and water. Bring

* For details see page 149.

to boil, stirring to keep from scorching and burning. Add water if needed. Let cook until creamy and thick. Serve with rice and/or whole wheat toast. (It's especially good with rice.)

Variations:

    1) Omit fenugreek and/or mustard seeds.

    2) For fenugreek and/or mustard seeds substitute 1 teaspoon garam masala (see note on page 54).

    3) Add 2 medium-ripe tomatoes (which have been scalded, peeled and mashed) just after adding the onion.

Quick Doshas

They look like crepes, but they're richer, simpler and more wholesome!

Prepare the following:
> Sort and wash 1 cup WASHED SPLIT MUNG DAHL in
> hot water.

Have on hand:
> ½ cup WATER
> ½ teaspoon SALT
> 1 teaspoon GHEE

Put uncooked, unsoaked dahl in blender with water and salt and blend until liquified. More water may be needed to make thin batter. Heat a heavy, iron frypan until very hot and put a small amount of ghee in the pan. Now pour part of the mung into the pan and spread over bottom extremely thin, (the thickness of crepes). Cook until slightly brown. A small saucer or bowl may be used to spread the batter, but it must be done quickly. Doshas must cook through and through so the mung will be digestible. Turn and cook on the other side. Add more ghee if necessary, but not enough to make it too greasy. Use remainder of batter in the same manner. Serve while hot with fresh chutney.*

---

* See Chapter X for recipes.

Soybean Dahl

A simple, quick way of preparing soybeans so that they are tender, sweet, delicious and melt in your mouth.

Prepare the following:
  Sort and wash 1½ cups SOYBEANS, soak at least overnight
    (36 to 48 hours is better). Drain and rinse thoroughly.
  Cut 2 medium ONIONS into ⅜ inch rings.
Have on hand:
  4 cups WATER
  1 tablespoon ground FENUGREEK
  4 tablespoons GHEE
  1½ teaspoons TURMERIC
  1½ teaspoons GROUND CUMIN
  1½ teaspoons GROUND CORIANDER
  1½ teaspoons SALT
  1 tablespoon BUTTER

  Put soybeans in pressure pot with water. Add fenugreek.
Bring to pressure and cook for 15 mintues. Let cool, open, drain
all water and wash beans thoroughly in boiling water. Take out
1 cup, mash it, and put it back in pot. Put ghee in large, heavy
iron frypan and heat on medium flame. Add turmeric, cumin
and coriander; fry until they begin to brown (not very dark). Add
onions and fry until onions begin to brown. Put drained, washed
soybeans back into pressure pot and add fried onions, rinsing out
pan with hot water. Add salt and butter. Cover with water the
depth of half the depth of the beans. (If beans come up 2 inches in
pot, put 1 inch of water over them.) Cover, bring to pressure and
cook for 10 minutes. Let cool, uncover and serve with rice.

Dahl on Top

A wonderful way to get vegetables and dahl all in one dish.
All it needs is rice or toast to make a complete meal.

Prepare the following:

Cut 2 medium ONIONS in ⅜ inch rings.

Cut 1 cup MUSHROOMS in ¼ inch pieces.

Cut 1 cup BROCCOLI florets and stem (peeled and thinly cut).

Cut 1 cup ZUCCHINI, GREEN BEANS, SPINACH or vegetable of your choice.

Sort and wash ½ cup WASHED SPLIT MUNG DAHL, soak for several hours (approximately 3 to 4). Drain and rinse thoroughly. Cook in water to cover about 2 inches over the beans. Cook about 10 to 15 minutes or until tender.

Have on hand:

4 tablespoons GHEE

1 teaspoon TURMERIC

1 teaspoon WHOLE CUMIN

1 teaspoon GROUND CUMIN

3 teaspoons GROUND CORIANDER

1 teaspoon BLACK MUSTARD SEED

1-1½ teaspoons SALT

WATER as needed

Put ghee in a large, heavy frypan and heat on medium flame. Add turmeric, cumin and coriander and fry until they begin to brown. Then add mustard seed and fry slowly until the seeds begin to pop but not explode like popcorn. Add the onions and fry until they begin to look translucent and of yellowing color (about 3-5 minutes). Then add mushrooms and fry about 3-5 minutes. You may cover the pan to help draw moisture from the vegetables. (This helps to steam them and prevent sticking and burning.) Next add other vegetables and fry for 3-5 minutes as above. Add salt (to taste) and water as needed. Cook about 20-30 minutes, covered only part of the time. When almost done and vegetables are boiling, put cooked dahl on top without stirring. Dahl should not touch bottom. A few minutes before cooking is complete, the dahl can be stirred in. Then turn off heat, cover and let steam a moment before serving. Serve with rice and/or whole wheat toast.

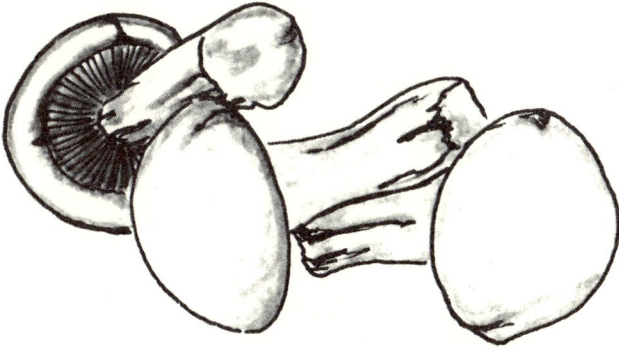

"Chocolate" Dahl

Of course it's not really chocolate, but it almost looks that way. A rich and meaty dahl.

Prepare the following:
  Sort and wash 1¼ cups WHOLE (GREEN) MUNG
    DAHL. Soak overnight, drain and rinse thoroughly.
  Cut 1 large ONION.
  Slice 1¼ cups MUSHROOMS ¼ inch thick.
  Cut 1 medium GREEN PEPPER into ½ inch pieces.
  Scald, peel and cube 1 large TOMATO.
  Flake 2 tablespoons BLANCHED ALMONDS.
Have on hand:
  About 6 cups WATER
  4-5 tablespoons GHEE
  1 teaspoon TURMERIC
  1 teaspoon WHOLE CUMIN
  1 teaspoon GROUND CUMIN
  3 teaspoons GROUND CORIANDER
  1 teaspoon BLACK MUSTARD SEED
  1½ teaspoons SALT

  Put soaked mung into a rather thin (but not aluminum)
pot with 3½ cups water. Cook over medium to high flame
(higher if pot is thicker). Let boil down until it begins scorching a
little on the bottom. Add boiling water and stir up from bottom
to get browned part into dahl. Let it cook down again and
brown on bottom. Add water and scrape loose. Continue to do
this until the mung is chocolate colored. Be sure it doesn't burn
because this will cause it to have a bitter taste.

Put ghee in a large, heavy iron frypan and heat on medium flame. Add turmeric, cumin and coriander and fry until cumin seeds begin to brown. Then add mustard seed and fry until seeds begin to pop. Add onions and fry until translucent then add mushrooms and green peppers and fry until dark brown. Add tomato and almonds and fry briefly. Put in beans, add salt (to taste) and cover with water. Let cook down on fairly high fire for 20-30 minutes adding boiling water when necessary and cover about half the time. Be sure to stir often enough to prevent sticking and burning. When it thickens and gains body it's ready to serve. If a thin pot and heavy frypan are used and the scorching process properly carried out, the dahl will have a good chocolate color. Otherwise it will be a lighter color but will still taste good.

Pakori

This is an unusual way to get your dahl and your protein but is quite delicious, perfect for parties and special occasions. A real treat (but don't do it every day).

Prepare the following:

Soak ¼ cup BLANCHED ALMONDS and ¼ cup CASHEWS for several hours.

Prepare FRESH SPINACH leaves by washing, shaking off surplus water and placing on paper towels to drain all water so batter will stick.

Sort and wash ½ cup WHOLE MUNG DAHL.

Have on hand:

2 teaspoons GROUND CORIANDER

4 teaspoons GROUND CUMIN

½ cup BESAN (gram flour)

1½ teaspoons SALT

2 cups GHEE

WATER

Put unsoaked, uncooked mung and 1 cup water in blender. Blend until smooth. Add besan and salt. Blend until smooth. Pour into a bowl. Put ⅛ to ¼ cup water and soaked (drained) nuts in blender without rinsing. Coarsely grind nuts and pour into bowl. Stir and mix well into a batter.

Put ghee in wok and heat until hot. Dip each spinach leaf in batter and deep fry in ghee. Turn leaf bottom side up and slip into ghee to keep batter from sliding off into ghee because it will burn and stick to others as they cook. Drain on paper towels. Better eaten while hot and crisp.

Mungocha

An unusual way to prepare mung. Perhaps for variety you will enjoy it.

Prepare the following:

Sort and wash 1 cup WHOLE MUNG DAHL, soak overnight, drain and rinse thoroughly.

Soak ¼ cup CASHEWS overnight.

Blend uncooked, presoaked whole mung in blender with equal amounts of water, 1 teaspoon WHOLE CUMIN and 2 teaspoons SALT.

Blend cashews into milk with 1 cup WATER.

Cut 2 medium ONIONS into thin slices and chop.

Have on hand:

3 tablespoons GHEE
1 teaspoon WHOLE CUMIN
SALT to taste

Put ghee in wok and heat on medium flame. Add whole cumin and fry until seeds are brown. Add onions and fry until they begin to brown. Pour part of pureed dahl into wok and cook down, stirring often enough to prevent burning. If it browns on bottom, stir and scrape the browned part into the dahl. This adds flavor. Continue to add blended dahl until all has been added and cook it down each time some is added. It should be cooked about 40-45 minutes. Then add cashew milk and salt and cook down until it becomes dry and crumbly. It is now ready to serve. Serve with chutney,* subzi (vegetable dish) and wheat-soy bread.

* See recipes for chutney in Chapter X.

Sweet and Sour Mung with Soy

Nina made the dahl—delicious but too watery. Swamiji thickened it with soy powder and what a happy accident!

Prepare the following:
>   Sort and wash 1¼ cups WASHED SPLIT MUNG DAHL,
>   soak for 3 or 4 hours, drain and rinse thoroughly.
>   Wash and chop 2 cups (packed) FRESH SPINACH.
>   Cut 2 small ONIONS in ⅜ inch rings.

Have on hand:
>   8 cups WATER
>   ⅛ cup RAW PEANUTS
>   1 teaspoon TURMERIC
>   1¼ teaspoons SALT
>   1 tablespoon RAW SUGAR
>   1 tablespoon LEMON JUICE
>   3 tablespoons GHEE
>   1 teaspoon CUMIN SEED
>   1 teaspoon BLACK MUSTARD SEED
>   1½ teaspoons grated FRESH GINGER
>   2 cups WATER
>   1 huge cooking spoon SOY POWDER

Put washed split mung dahl in pot and add 6 cups water, raw peanuts, turmeric, salt, sugar and lemon juice and cook for about 1 hour. Be sure to add boiling water if necessary.

Meanwhile, put ghee in a large, heavy, iron frypan and heat on medium flame. Add cumin seed, mustard seed, fresh ginger and fry slowly until brown. Add onions and fry until quite brown. Add spinach and fry briefly. Then put this in pot with mung. Add 2 cups boiling water and 1 huge cooking spoon soy powder. Stir well and allow to cook over low heat for at least ½ hour. It must be stirred frequently after the soy powder has been added to prevent sticking. This is creamy, rich and a little sweet. It is very delicious served with rice and at the same meal with mustard-paneer vegetables* and chapatis. It may be too sweet for some tastes; if so, the amount of sugar can be reduced.

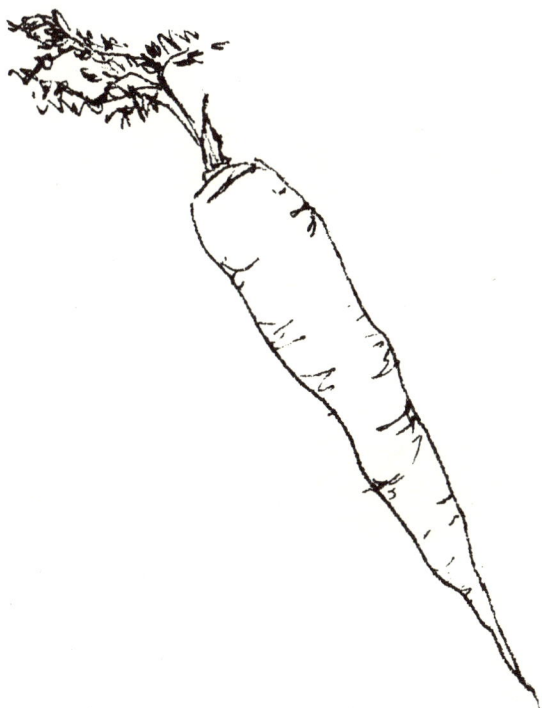

* See page 70 for recipe.

Chana Stew with Nuts

This is another one that "sticks to your ribs." Crunchy too.

Prepare the following:
  Sort and wash ¾ cup CHANA (dark "shriveled" chick peas), soak at least overnight. (Soaking 36 to 48 hours is better.) Drain and rinse thoroughly. Cook in water to cover about 2 inches over the beans, with cover cracked for about 1-1½ hours. Be sure water does not boil out and peas burn. Add boiling water if necessary.
Meanwhile, prepare the following:
  Cut 1 large ONION into ⅜ inch rings.
  Slice 1-1½ cups MUSHROOMS into ¼ inch slices.
  Chop 1 large GREEN PEPPER into ½ inch squares.
  Cut small (5-6 inch) ZUCCHINI into ¼ inch rings and quarter.
  Cut 1½-2 cups BROCCOLI keeping florets bite-size, peel and cut stems very thin.
  Wash, drain and chop 2 cups FRESH SPINACH.
  Blanch ⅛ cup ALMONDS and halve.
  Measure ¼ cup PINE NUTS.
Have on hand:
  4 tablespoons GHEE
  1 teaspoon TURMERIC
  1 teaspoon WHOLE CUMIN
  1 teaspoon GROUND CUMIN
  3 teaspoons GROUND CORIANDER
  5 teaspoons BESAN (gram flour)
  1 pint YOGURT
  2 teaspoons SALT
  ⅛ to ¼ teaspoon RED PEPPER
  2 cups WATER

Put ghee in a large, heavy, iron frypan and heat on medium flame. Add turmeric, cumin, and coriander and fry until brown. Next, add onions and fry until most of the water fries out and they look yellowish (about 5 minutes). Continue to add in order prepared and fry each vegetable about 3 minutes before adding the next one. Add vegetables to chana in a large saucepan. Then add besan (chick pea flour or gram flour), yogurt, nuts, salt and pepper. Mix well, add about 2 cups water and cook over medium flame, first covered, then uncovered, alternately. Cook 1 hour, adding water when necessary and stirring to prevent sticking. The peas and nuts have a tendency to go to the bottom and stick, so be sure to stir often enough and from the bottom. Heat may be reduced somewhat after about 30 minutes. Dahl will not be extremely tender. Serve with rice and/or whole wheat toast.

Garbanzo Stew

Our relatives thought it was beef stew. It's not. The taste is a little bit different and a lot better. Your stomach will be pleased with it too, and it won't complain of hunger for a long time afterwards.

Prepare the following:

Sort and wash ¾ cup dried GARBANZOS. Soak at least overnight (36 to 48 hours is better.) Drain and rinse thoroughly. Put in saucepan and fill with water to cover about 2 inches over the beans and bring to boil. Lower flame and cook slowly with lid cracked for about 2 hours or until beans can be crushed between fingers. More boiling water may be needed, so check to prevent burning.

Meanwhile:

Cut 1 medium to large ONION in ⅜ inch rings.

Chop ¾-1 large GREEN PEPPER finely.

Cut 1 small hot BANANA PEPPER finely.

Cut 1-1½ six to eight inch ZUCCHINI into small pieces.

Cook 1 small POTATO and cube.

Have on hand:

3 tablespoons GHEE

1 teaspoon TURMERIC

1 teaspoon GROUND CUMIN

¼ teaspoon WHOLE CUMIN

2 teaspoons GROUND CORIANDER

1 small pinch GROUND CLOVES

⅛ teaspoon GROUND CINNAMON

⅛ teaspoon BLACK MUSTARD SEEDS

1½ teaspoons SALT

Put ghee in large, heavy, iron frypan and heat on medium flame. Add turmeric, cumin, coriander, cloves and cinnamon and fry on slow heat until very brown. Add mustard seeds and fry until they begin to pop. Then add onions and fry until translucent. Add peppers and fry until quite brown. Next add zucchini and cook briefly adding a little water if necessary to prevent sticking. Take 2 tablespoons of garbanzos and mash and add along with others.

Put everything into a large dutch oven and add salt and boiling water. Cook covered and uncovered, alternately, for about 1½ hours, adding hot water only as necessary and stirring occasionally to prevent sticking. About ½ hour before the end of cooking time, add cubed potato. By the end of cooking time, only beans are left with a thick, brown gravy. Serve with rice and/or with toast.

VIII
Breads

VIII Breads

Bread is perhaps one of the most ancient and basic items in the diet of man after he became a grower instead of a hunter and gatherer. When we say "bread" in the West, we usually mean something made out of wheat, and this is often what is meant throughout much of the world, especially in northern India. In other parts of India the bread is made from many different substances and exactly what ingredients are used and the quality, texture and type of bread depends on the customs, climate and availability of food in each local area. There are probably hundreds of different "breads" or *roti* eaten in India.

The most basic of all, however, and the most common is the *chapati*. This is the simplest and quickest form of bread that can be imagined. It is similar to other basic, traditional, simple breads throughout the world, like the *pita* of the Middle East, or like the *tortilla* of Mexico (which is made with corn,however.) Essentially the chapati is nothing more than a pancake-like circle of dough made from wheat and water, which is patted out, or rolled out, and thrown onto a hot griddle where it is "baked" until done. For the basic chapati the ingredients are only flour and water. Nothing else is added; it's even cooked on a dry griddle. The amount of heat and, therefore, fuel which is required is very little, since it cooks almost instantly. This is a great blessing in the hotter sections of India, where the temperature may climb above a hundred in the shade. Here chapatis are cooked on *angithis,* little squat mud or concrete vessels which contain hot coals and on which a dished-out, cast iron griddle is set. The fuel is put inside this, lit and fanned until it forms hot coals; meanwhile the dough is kneaded, allowed to sit for a short while, pulled into little balls which are rolled out into thin, flat chapatis. These are thrown on the hot griddle, turned over, and, afterwards, they are usually thrown directly onto the hot coals, which causes the already half-cooked patties to puff up like a balloon. This is considered the mark that the chapati is properly cooked. If the flour and water have been mixed in proper proportions, kneaded the right length of time, if the chapati has been tossed on the fire where it puffs up, and if the flour was fresh, you will have a most fragrant, tender and delicious sort of bread that is a joy and delight to chew.

While it remains the basic bread in much of India, there are many, many variations of this basic chapati, or *roti*. One variation is called *parantha*. In this case the chapati is dabbed with ghee, folded, dabbed again, folded again and finally rolled out a second time into a triangular sort of shape. In order to cook it well, a little clarified butter or ghee is spooned around the edges and allowed to soak in. As a result, it is almost fried, and it is heavier. *Paranthas* are most often used for special occasions, or by those given to richer food. But the *parantha* has an advantage, in that the ghee helps preserve it and seal in the moisture. Therefore a *parantha* made early in the morning can be carried in a lunch box until late in the day, and maintains its tenderness and flavor; whereas a chapati is not very good an hour after it's made, since it dries out and becomes tough and difficult to chew.

Another form of *roti*, which is deep fried, is called *puri*. These are like fritters, and are very popular for family gatherings and other celebrations. In some parts of India the *angithi* is larger and has a space inside in which the *roti* can be stuck against the inside wall, where it will more or less bake. This device is called a *tandoor*, and is especially popular among the Muslims. But more fuel is required and more heat is produced. It was perhaps suited to the Muslim invaders from Afghanistan, but less so to South Indians. When the English came in the last century, they introduced the European-style bread which was given a name appropriately half English and half Hindi: "double roti" because it was much thicker than the Indian roti. In urban centers in India, European-style bakeries will be found and the bread that is produced is usually quite delicious since the processing, bleaching and chemicalizing of the flour has not been adopted in India, where the added cost of industrial equipment to do this would make the bread prohibitively expensive.

Yeast-raised loaf bread, while it was a novelty to the people who live in the plains of India, has been prepared in the mountains for ages. In the Himalayas, where the weather is cold much of the year, it is common to have fires built and enough heat produced to bake bread. The baking is commonly done with heated stones, and the product is called a "stone cake." The best results are obtained by putting the bread between two heated stones and allowing them to cook it. A variation is the "leaf cake" (see recipe that follows). Here, tender, fragrant leaves of the local trees are used to protect the bread from being scorced by the stones, and the leaves impart a unique flavor and aroma to the bread.

Another variation is called "ground cake." In this case, a hole is dug in the ground, a fire is built in it, and when the soil has become quite hot, the bread dough is put into the hole and the opening in the ground is covered. After some time the bread is dug up, and a football-sized loaf, which is light and fluffy, emerges!

The Hindu Loaf for which we give a recipe here, is so-called by the Muslims, who are generally meat eaters. The Hindu Loaf, though it is based on wheat, contains its own complement of legumes (beans and peas) as well as seeds and nuts. This makes it a very high-quality, complete protein, and is a meat substitute for the Hindus. It's not really a bread in the usual sense, though we include it here; it is rather a "loaf," a main dish, very meaty and satisfying, and can be served simply with a light vegetable for added vitamins and minerals.

Many other grains and legumes are used to make different bread-like dishes in India. *Makkai-ki-roti* is a sort of chapati made out of corn meal, maise having been brought from America to India by way of Europe. It has become quite popular in the Punjab, and near the foothills of the Himalayas, where, when combined with mustard greens, it is considered a delicacy.

Another roti popular in the colder areas is *bajara-ki-roti,* another flat bread or chapati-like bread made from a dark grey millet. This variety of millet has the special property of creating warmth and drying the body, and when taken with ghee and gur, it is guite delicious and healthful in the cooler rainy seasons.

In the mountains a *dosha* is sometimes made from mung dahl (see section on dahls). Doshas are a South Indian bread-like dish, which look like pancakes. In the South, they are generally made out of a mixture of rice and dahl. This is a very good combination because of the protein that results.[1]

[1] In other cases, when using wheat flour in the making of roti, a leguminous flour such as besan, which is the flour made from chana dahl (chick peas) may be mixed in small portions before kneading to complement the grain and create a complete protein.

Chapatis

This is a basic recipe. With practice you will turn out a perfect chapati. And when your fingers become nimble like the Indian cooks, you will find it's fun too.

Prepare the following:
    1 cup WHOLE WHEAT FLOUR
    ½ cup WATER

Put flour in bowl. Make a hole in the middle and add the water slowly, mixing well. Knead until dough is springy (about 10-15 minutes). To test, make print with finger and see if dough springs out. Indent top with finger and fill holes with water. Cover and let stand for about 30 minutes (if time permits).

Take a small amount and shape like a biscuit. Flour sides and roll out very thin and about size of a large pancake. Place on a hot, dry griddle or in a hot, heavy, iron frypan. It will begin to puff in spots. If pan is not hot enough, it will only dry out and not puff. Let cook until dotted with light brown spots. Turn and cook on other side. Remove from pan and throw on flame top side down first until it puffs all over. Must keep moving and turning to prevent burning. May butter if desire. Clean pan to remove burned flour before cooking another. Best if served while hot.

Crisp Chapatis

Almost like crackers for those who like crunchy, crisp bread.

Have on hand:
    2 cups WHOLE WHEAT FLOUR
    2/3 cup MILK
    GHEE

Put flour in a bowl. Make an indentation in the flour and add milk very slowly, working it into the flour with fingers. (A little ghee on fingers helps keep flour from sticking to them.) Knead very well—for at least 10-15 minutes. (If left to stand awhile, be sure to cover.) Take enough dough to roll a very thin cake the size of bottom of heavy, iron skillet in which they're to be cooked. Heat skillet, put in small amount of ghee, throw in cake and while cooking puncture rapidly all over until well covered with small lines. When cooked on this side, turn and cook in same manner on other side. The puncturing takes out the air and thus makes it crisp. These may be stored for several days. They keep well, but are better if served while hot.

Paranthas

These are a special treat. A bit too rich for daily eating.

Have on hand:
   1½ cups WHOLE WHEAT FLOUR
   About ½ cup COLD WATER
   GHEE

   Put flour into mixing bowl. Make indentation in center
and pour in cold water a little at a time, working it into a dough.
It will require almost ½ cup cold water, but don't make it too
soft. Knead for about 10-15 minutes. Test it by punching it
lightly with finger and if it springs back, it's ready. Take enough
dough to make a ball a little larger than a golf ball. Pat between
the hands until it's smooth and round. Grease counter top with
ghee. Place dough on counter top and roll until it's about ⅛ inch
thick. With fingers, spread a little ghee on half, doubling it over.
Then with fingers put a little ghee on half of this and fold over.
Then roll this out until it's about ⅛ inch thick. Heat heavy, iron
frypan to medium-high heat and put rolled dough in. Put a little
ghee around edges as it cooks. Let it cook until under side is
brown. Turn and brown other side, putting ghee around the
edges. Press on it while it's browning. This makes a delicious
flaky parantha. Serve with subzi (vegetables).

Bajara Bran Muffins

Bajara is wonderful enough to deserve more attention. Here is a way of working it into a Western dish.

Prepare the following:
 Measure 1 cup BAJARA FLOUR.
 Measure ¼ cup WHOLE WHEAT FLOUR.
 Measure 1 cup ALL-BRAN CEREAL.
 Measure 1 tablespoon RUMFORD'S BAKING POWDER.
 Measure ¼ teaspoon SALT.
 Measure 3 tablespoons of SORGHUM and 1 tablespoon of
   MOLASSES.
 Measure 1¼ cups MILK.
 Measure ¼ cup GHEE.
 1 EGG.

 Stir together flour (both kinds), baking powder, salt and set aside. Place All-Bran and milk in mixing bowl, stir to combine and let stand 1 or 2 minutes or until cereal is softened. Add egg, sorghum, molasses and ghee and beat well. Add dry ingredients to cereal mixture, stirring only until combined. Portion batter evenly into 12 greased 2½ inch muffin pan cups. Bake in oven at 400° F. about 25 minutes or until muffins are golden brown. Serve hot.

Wheat-Soy Bread

Simple, basic and wholesome. The combination of wheat and soy makes an excellent protein.

Prepare the following:

Measure 3 cups WHOLE WHEAT FLOUR.

Measure ¾ cup SOY POWDER.

Put ½ package YEAST in ¼ cup WARM (not hot) WATER.

Have on hand:

GHEE

PISTACHIO NUTS

Place flour and soy powder in mixing bowl. Make indentation in center and add yeast and then water (enough to make a springy, not too soft, dough) gradually until blends into dough. Knead for about 10 or 15 minutes until it is springy. Test it by gently pressing with a finger, and if it springs back it's OK. Now pat out to fit an 8 x 8 inch pan. Place in pan which has been slightly greased with ghee. Then sprinkle with pistachios. Place in preheated 450° oven and bake for about 25-30 minutes. Then lower temperature to 150°, pour ghee over it and bake for 10 minutes. Serve with subzi (vegetable dish).

Variation: Substitute 2 cups oat flour and 1 cup barley flour for 3 cups whole wheat flour.

Leftover bread: Wrap well in dishtowel. Keep in a well-ventilated, cool place. If it dries out too hard to eat, put in a pot with 1 teaspoon ghee in which a few cashews and raisins have been fried. Cover well with milk and water (4 to 1 ratio) and bring to a boil. Simmer at least an hour. It will swell to a dumpling-like consistency. Serve alone or topped with honey.

Oopma

This is a halwa that's not sweet and, as with halwa, there are many variations. Make it light, make it dark, cook it long, cook it short. This one is called "Masala Oopma."

Prepare the following:
    Grate 1 small ONION.
    Measure ½ cup SOOJI.*
    Cut small ½ cup BROCCOLI FLORETS.
    Thaw ½ cup frozen GREEN PEAS.
    Halve 1 tablespoon CASHEWS.
Have on hand:
    4 tablespoons GHEE
    1 teaspoon TURMERIC
    1 teaspoon WHOLE CUMIN
    1 teaspoon GROUND CUMIN
    3 teaspoons GROUND CORIANDER
    1 teaspoon BLACK MUSTARD SEED
    about 1 pint HOT WATER
    1 teaspoon SALT

Put ghee in a wok on medium-high flame. Add turmeric, cumin and coriander, and fry until they begin to brown. Then add mustard seed and fry until seeds begin to pop. Add sooji and fry until light brown. Add grated onion and continue to fry until sooji is a golden brown. Add broccoli, green peas, cashews and 1 pint of hot water. (Keep a pot of hot water nearby to add as it cooks down.) Continue to cook until all water evaporates. Add

---

* Sooji is a fine, cracked wheat similar to cream of wheat but whole grain. It is available in most Indian food stores.

more water and the salt and let it cook down. Be sure to scrape down from the sides of the wok during cooking, so grains will not burn and spoil the taste. If some browns on bottom, scrape into the mixture as it adds flavor, but be careful not to let it burn. Continue to add water and cook down until sooji is soft and creamy and gets a shiny look as though it's giving up the ghee. Continue to cook down until it becomes crumbly. Then it's ready to serve.

Leaf Cake

We like to use maple leaves, but you may choose your own flavor.

Have on hand:
  ¾ cup MILK
  ¼ cup WATER
  1 package YEAST
  2 tablespoons RAW SUGAR
  2½ cups WHOLE WHEAT FLOUR
  ¼ cup chopped CASHEWS
  ¼ cup KISHMISH (white raisins)
  GHEE
  MAPLE, GRAPE, BANANA, MANGO, FIG or BANYON
  LEAVES

Put milk and water in saucepan and heat to yeast-dissolving temperature. Be sure it's not too hot because the yeast will be killed. Add yeast and dissolve. Then add raw sugar and dissolve. Mix this with whole wheat flour and knead for five minutes. Allow to rise covered for about 30 minutes. Punch down and roll out slightly more than half (with ghee, not flour) to shape of pan and cover with ghee. Then sprinkle with chopped cashews and kishmish.

Roll remainder of dough slightly smaller than bottom. Place on top and roll edges of bottom over the top to seal. Cover on both sides with ghee and then with leaves. Place in heavy, iron frypan, well greased with ghee. Cover and cook on medium to high heat, adding ghee if necessary. Leaves protect from direct heat and provide moisture which steams cake. It will rise. Leaves may smell as though they're burning because they will be parched but they can be peeled from the cake before serving.

Cook until leaves on underside are parched. Turn, add ghee and cook on other side until leaves are parched and cake seems done. You may test it with a straw to see if it has cooked through. Peel leaves from the cake and serve. To serve leftover cake, boil in milk until moist and soft. Then serve.

Himalayan Pizza

People sometimes tell me, "After I improve my diet, I've really missed pizza. But when I go back and have some, I'm always disappointed. It tastes like cardboard." This recipe is for them. They won't be disappointed.

Prepare the following:

Mince very fine 2 medium ONIONS.

Mince 1½ cups MUSHROOMS.

Mince very fine 1 cup GREEN PEPPER.

Mince very fine 1 cup ZUCCHINI.

Scald, peel and mash 6-8 medium very ripe TOMATOES.

Have on hand:

4 tablespoons GHEE

1 teaspoon TURMERIC

1 teaspoon WHOLE CUMIN

1 teaspoon GROUND CUMIN

3 teaspoons GROUND CORIANDER

1 teaspoon BLACK MUSTARD SEED

1¼ teaspoons SALT

1 cup MILK

1/16 teaspoon RED PEPPER

⅛ teaspoon BLACK PEPPER

2¾ cups WHOLE WHEAT FLOUR

¾ cup MILK

1 package DRY YEAST

¼ cup WARM (not hot) WATER

about ¼ cup chopped RAW CASHEWS or flaked
  ALMONDS

GHEE

Put ghee in a large, heavy, iron frypan and heat on medium flame. Add turmeric, whole cumin, ground cumin, coriander and fry until seeds begin to brown. Then add mustard seed and fry slowly until dark brown and mustard seeds begin to pop. Add the onions and fry until the onions begin to turn yellow and translucent. Then add the mushrooms and fry 3-5 minutes covered part of the time to help bring out moisture which will steam them and prevent burning. Next add green pepper and fry 3-5 minutes covered part of the time. Do the same with the zucchini. Add the tomatoes and salt. Cover and let simmer until thick enough to spread on crust (about 30 minutes) stirring often enough to prevent sticking. Add milk, red pepper, black pepper. Let simmer uncovered until it thickens again (10-15 minutes). Put aside. This is the subzi topping.

Meanwhile, dissolve yeast in warm water. Mix flour, milk and yeast into a springy dough. Knead until, when pressed lightly with a finger, dough will spring back (about 10-15 minutes). Cover and let stand 15-20 minutes to rise. Then roll out slightly more than half of it on a counter greased with ghee. Put this in pan heavily greased with ghee and covered with maple leaves (if available) which will help to steam it. Smear with ¼-½ inch of the subzi (vegetable dish) which was prepared. Sprinkle with chopped cashews or flaked almonds. Roll out remainder of dough, place on top and seal edges by rolling bottom crust over top. Put ghee or skimmings from making ghee on top. Bake at 350°-375° F. until brown (about 45 minutes). Serve hot.

Hindu Loaf

This dish is primarily soy flour, sunflower seeds and whole wheat flour. Besides being quite delicious, it is a highly concentrated form of protein. It can be kept in the refrigerator for several days, and leftover slices fried (and served with grits—if you're from the South and miss your sausage and grits).

Prepare the following:
Mince fine 1 medium ONION.
Mince fine 1 medium GREEN PEPPER.
Puree ½ cup fresh MUSHROOMS* in ½ cup WATER.
Put ½ package (1 piling teaspoon) DRY YEAST in ⅛ cup
   WARM (not hot) WATER and dissolve.
Have on hand:
1 cup WHOLE WHEAT FLOUR
¾ cup GROUND SUNFLOWER SEEDS†
1/3 cup GROUND ALMONDS†
⅝ cup SOY FLOUR
½ teaspoon GROUND CUMIN
1 teaspoon GROUND CORIANDER
1 teaspoon SALT
1 teaspoon BLACK PEPPER
3 tablespoons GHEE
1⅛ cups WATER

* If time is limited, onions and green pepper may be blended with mushrooms. Loaf may be a little more moist but still delicious.

† For this we use a little electric coffee mill and nut grinder—but the seeds and nuts can be thrown in the blender with the other ingredients and "pureed."

Dissolve yeast in warm water. Stir together whole wheat flour, sunflower seed, almonds, soy flour, cumin, coriander, salt, pepper and ghee. Add 1⅛ cups water and yeast and mix. Then add minced onions, minced green peppers, pureed mushrooms and blend into a thick batter. Pour into a well-greased (with ghee) heavy, iron frypan. Bake at 400° for 15 minutes. Lower temperature to 375° and bake for 35 minutes. Turn off heat and leave in oven awhile (about 10 minutes). It's almost like a souffle. Serve as soon as possible.

Loaf

This is a similar loaf to the last one, though a little less Hindu: eggs are added, which makes it lighter and a bit richer.

Prepare the following:
  ¾ cups GROUND SUNFLOWER SEED.*
  1¼ cups GROUND CASHEWS, ALMONDS* or nuts of
  choice, leaving some larger pieces.
  Chop very fine 2-2½ small ONIONS (about 1½ cups).
  Chop very fine ¾ medium-large GREEN PEPPER (1 cup).
  Chop very fine 10 medium MUSHROOMS (about 1¾
  cups).
  Melt 1 stick BUTTER.
  Put 1½ piling teaspoons YEAST in 1 1/3 cups warm water
  (not hot), cover and let stand.
  Beat well 3 EGGS.
Have on hand:
  1¼ cups WHOLE WHEAT FLOUR
  9/10 cup SOY FLOUR
  1¼ teaspoons SALT
  ⅛ teaspoon GROUND PEPPER
  GHEE

Mix flours, ground seeds and nuts. Add melted butter, eggs and warm water with yeast and stir until a thick batter is formed. Add onions, green pepper, mushrooms, salt and pepper to taste. Pour into a well-greased (with ghee), heavy, iron frypan. Bake in 350° preheated oven for 45-50 minutes. Then turn off heat and let soak about 15 minutes. Serve as soon as possible with your favorite subzi (vegetable dish).

* See second footnote on p. 140.

IX
Dairy

IX Dairy

Milk is extremely important in the Indian diet. The Hindu's reverence for the cow stems from his recognition that it supplies him with some of his most valuable and indispensable nutrition. When I inquired about the prohibition against killing cows, I was told with surprise, "But you wouldn't harm your mother who gives you milk!" Cows are found everywhere in India, sleeping in a lean-to by the house, or wandering down the street. They enjoy a very privileged position and seem quite content and confident. Even in the midst of busy traffic, they never have a frightened or startled look. If it is true that the best milk comes from contented cows, then perhaps this is why milk is so delicious in India. The care given the cow makes good nutritional sense.

In the plains, however, much of the milk comes from the water buffalo. This milk is more cooling, heavier, and quite white in color. It's high in butterfat, and quite delicious; but not as light as the cow's milk. In much of India goat milk is also very popular, and excellent breeds of milk goats are available. Goat milk is less fattening and creates less mucus.

In the mountains cows are more common than water buffalo, and cow milk is a staple. Much of the diet is organized around milk and milk products.

Clarified butter, or ghee of course, is the basis of most Indian recipes; and though vegetable oils are used in the south, in the north this practice is little adopted. Though in the West it has been said that vegetable oils are less likely to cause hardening of the arteries, research has not borne this out.* Studies of the Indian diet have shown heart attacks to be less frequent in the areas where ghee is used most heavily. According to the medical writings of ancient India, ghee has many marvelous properties, and is highly regarded both as a nutrient and as a preservative for foods and medicines. A dish cooked in ghee will retain its freshness and nutritional value much longer. Furthermore, it is thought that the ghee takes up the nutrients and their qualities and carries them into the body.

In India as soon as the milk is brought in from milking, it is boiled. This is always and invariably done, as it is felt it makes the milk clean and improves its digestibility. After the boiling, many different things can be done with the milk. First of all the cream which comes to the top is skimmed off. To this is usually added a little bit of yogurt, so that it will sour slightly and from it butter is made and later ghee.

The plain milk is used as an ingredient in many dishes, or it may be drunk hot, served straight from the boiling pot. Where there is no refrigeration, and especially in the warmer areas of India, it is difficult to prevent the milk from spoiling.

One way of preserving the milk is to culture it, so that the bacteria that grows in it will be helpful rather than harmful. This process is called making yogurt (see recipe that follows) and yogurt is a favorite dish of the Indians. It is taken either plain or used as an ingredient in many recipes. It is considered to be especially good when it is mixed with honey or when it is served with mung dahl.

Another way of using the milk so that it will not spoil is to make *paneer* or fresh cheese. In this case lemon juice is added straight to the boiling milk so that it curdles. This is then strained and a fresh, delicious cheese, somewhat like cottage cheese, though lighter to digest, results. The liquid that comes out, the

---

* For details see Chapter V of *Diet and Nutrition* by Rudolph Ballentine, M.D., published by the Himalayan Institute.

"whey," is often used because of its marvelous cleansing properties. It is considered especially good for the kidneys and bladder (see recipe for *paneer* that follows).

Many sweets are also made from milk, and this often is based on *khoya* (see recipe that follows), a condensed, or boiled down, or evaporated form of milk, that is quite custardy and heavy. Many forms of this are made, and the result is a concentrated milk that will not spoil. For instance, sugar is added to the *khoya* and this is cooked down until it becomes a sort of candy called *burfi*. While the sugar may not be very nutritious, the milk certainly is, and the sugar protects it from spoiling.

While soybeans are mentioned in the ancient writings, their use has been rather limited until recent years, except in the mountains. However, the making of soy milk is not uncommon now even in the plains of India. Its cheese, *tofu*, can be used in much the same way as *paneer* (see recipes that follow for tofu and soy milk). In the Himalayas, tofu was made by curdling the milk with sour yogurt or very tart fruit juices, while in Japan, *nigari*, an extract of seawater, is used. Bean "dairy" products, like tofu, have many of the advantages of milk, plus many that milk does not possess. They are lighter and less likely to create mucus in the body. Moreover, they are much cheaper and practical, since a container of soy beans can provide milk for weeks without requiring room for a cow, pasture, and all of the other difficulties that make it so problematic to supply people with enough dairy milk.

Ghee

Place 1 pound UNSALTED BUTTER in a saucepan. Heat until it boils. Then lower heat. Do not have flame too high because it will burn on bottom before water boils out. Foam will accumulate on top. When it begins to collapse and thicken, start skimming while it continues to boil. This will remove the milky portion of the butter. Do not stir up from the bottom as some of the milky portion settles. It can be scraped from the pot after pouring off the ghee. Be careful that this does not scorch and ruin the taste. These solids which remain in the bottom should only brown slightly. You will know that it is ready when all the water boils out and only the clear oily part remains. (The oily part is the ghee.) Turn the heat off and let ghee sit for a moment. During this time the hot fat will begin to turn the sediment in the bottom a golden brown color. Then the ghee can be poured off into an earthenware or metal vessel. If the sediment turns black, it means that the ghee was overheated, and this will damage it. The skimmings may be saved and added to vegetables for flavor.

Yogurt

Once you get the hang of it, it's quite easy to do. Homemade yogurt (if it is made from a good culture) is much more healthful than that which is bought in the store. It's also incredibly cheaper.

For 1 quart, pour 1 quart MILK into saucepan and bring to boil. Let cool to 105-110° and add CULTURE (may purchase at health food store with instructions on package or borrow about two tablespoons of yogurt from a friend for culture) dissolved in a little cooled milk. (Be sure it's cooled or culture will be killed.) Stir until well mixed. Pour into jar, wrap in dish towel and place in warm place or place jar in warm water (about 105-110°) which covers jar to top but not over top. Keep water at even temperature until yogurt is made. Let stand about 4-5 hours depending upon warmth of place. Be sure it's warm enough but not too hot. Check at intervals by tilting jar to see if it has thickened and will slip from side of jar. If so, it is done and is ready to be placed in refrigerator where it will gel when cooled. Be sure to save enough yogurt to be used for the next culture (about 2 tablespoons per quart). To make more yogurt, boil as many quarts of milk as desired. Let cool to 105-110°, add 2 tablespoons yogurt of first batch to some of the cooled milk. Then proceed as above, except keep closer watch on it. It should be done in about 2 hours. Be sure not to let it stand too long because taste will then be tarter. For sweet, mellow yogurt it must be refrigerated at proper time.

After it has "ripened" in refrigerator 6-8 hours it is better. Then it may be served with a little honey stirred in.

Paneer

This beats commercial cottage cheese by a mile. It's also less fattening, more easily digested and has a much fresher taste. Don't throw away the liquid that comes out (whey). A cup of it every other day or so keeps the body clean and helps the urinary system function properly.

Have on hand:
   ½ gallon MILK
   Juice of 2 LEMONS

   For about 1 cup, put milk in saucepan or wok and bring to boil. Add juice of 1 lemon for each quart of milk. Stir and allow to boil another few seconds. When curdled, strain through thin cloth (cheesecloth or thin dishtowel) and squeeze all liquid out until desired consistency. Should be very dry if it is to be cut into squares for vegetable dishes, but not too dry if to be used like cottage or cream cheese.

Variation: If paneer is to be used for cheese cake, add less lemon juice so paneer will not be as tight and will cream more easily and quickly.

Cheese Cake

Indian paneer dressed up American style.

Have on hand:
  1 1/3 cups GRAHAM CRACKER CRUMBS
  ¼ cup GHEE
  2 or 3 LEMONS
  1 gallon MILK
  5 tablespoons LIGHT HONEY
  3 EGG YOLKS
  5 teaspoons LEMON JUICE
Topping:
  2 or 3 tablespoons LIGHT HONEY
  1 cup SOUR CREAM

Put graham cracker crumbs in pyrex pie dish. Add ghee (more if necessary) and spread to form crust. Put in 350° oven and bake for 10 minutes. Set aside to cool. Squeeze lemons. Put milk in large saucepan and bring to boil. Using only enough lemon juice to pull all curd from whey, pour it into hot milk and stir once. When curdled, pour into strainer lined with thin cloth (cheesecloth or dishtowel) and press until curds are about consistency of cottage cheese.* This is paneer. Put cheese (paneer) in blender, add honey and blend. When cool, add egg yolks and blend until well mixed. Next add lemon juice to taste and blend well. Pour this in cooled crust.

Sour Cream Topping (optional): Mix honey and sour cream. Spread on top and it's ready to serve.

---

* For details see recipe on page 150.

Peas Paneer

One of the aristocrats of Indian vegetable dishes.

Prepare the following:

    Make Paneer* using 2 quarts MILK (2% best) and juice of 2 LEMONS.

    Scald, peel and crush 6 small or 4 medium TOMATOES.

    Cut 2 cups ONION RINGS ⅜ inch thick.

    Chop 1 cup MUSHROOMS.

    Prepare 1 pound shelled fresh GREEN PEAS or thaw frozen green peas.

Have on hand:

    1¼ teaspoons TURMERIC

    2 teaspoons GROUND CUMIN

    3 teaspoons GROUND CORIANDER

    1 teaspoon BLACK MUSTARD SEED

    1½ teaspoons SALT

    3-4 tablespoons GHEE

    ⅛ teaspoon GROUND RED PEPPER

    Put peas in pressure pot and add tomatoes, cubed paneer, 1 teaspoon turmeric, the cumin, coriander, mustard seed, salt and hot water to cover. Cover, bring to pressure and cook for 7-10 minutes depending on size of peas.

    Meanwhile, saute onions in ghee in a heavy, iron frypan. Add ¼ teaspoon turmeric and fry until onions are translucent. Add mushrooms and fry until nearly black. Add to pressure pot along with red pepper and simmer uncovered for 10-15 minutes. Ready to serve. Serve with whole wheat toast.

---

* For instructions, see recipe on page 150.

Chowder
(Made from leftover PEAS PANEER)

Peas Paneer is good enough to make a lot, and if you manage to have some left over, you will be delighted with this way of serving it.

Prepare the following:

Sort for stones and liquify ½ cup dry WHOLE MUNG in blender with just enough water to blend.

Dice 3 small ONIONS.

Have on hand:

1½ cups leftover PEAS PANEER

4 cups MILK

2-3 tablespoons GHEE

1 teaspoon TURMERIC

2 teaspoons GROUND CUMIN

3 teaspoons GROUND CORIANDER

⅛ teaspoon GROUND RED PEPPER

Put leftover peas paneer in large saucepan. Add liquified mung beans and milk and then cook. Be sure to stir enough to prevent sticking.

Meanwhile, put ghee in a large, heavy frypan and heat on medium flame. Add turmeric, cumin and coriander and fry until light brown. Then add onions and fry until they begin to brown. Add this and the red pepper to the saucepan with peas paneer and mung and continue to cook until color develops and it's creamy. Serve as chowder with whole wheat toast.

Paneer Supreme

Here is a typical recipe based on paneer. If you try it, you will be making regular trips to the grocery store for milk and lemons.

Prepare the following:

Scald, peel and mash 2 medium to large TOMATOES.

Slice 2 medium ONIONS in rings ¼ inch thick.

Chop ½ medium GREEN PEPPER in ½ inch squares.

Cut 1-1½ cups BROCCOLI slicing stem very thin and leaving florets intact and bite-size. (Keep stems and florets separate.)

Cut 1½-2 cups MUSHROOMS in halves or quarters according to size.

Slice 1 ten-inch ZUCCHINI in slices ⅜ inch thick.

Make PANEER* using 2 quarts of MILK and 2 LEMONS.

Have on hand:

3 tablespoons GHEE

1½ teaspoons TURMERIC

2 teaspoons GROUND CORIANDER

½ teaspoon BLACK MUSTARD SEED

3 pinches of Baedecker's GARAM MASALA†

1 teaspoon SALT

about 5 tablespoons GHEE

---

* See recipe on page 150.

† A combination of spices. Can be purchased in most Indian grocery stores.

Put 3 tablespoons ghee in a very large, heavy, iron frypan and heat on medium heat. Add turmeric and coriander. Cook a short while and add black mustard seed. Fry until spices are dark brown. Add garam masala. Then add the tomatoes and cook until most of the broth has cooked out and it begins to fry, but be very careful that it doesn't burn. Add onions, mushrooms and green pepper and fry until all are tender. If mixture begins to stick add ghee or a small amount of water. Add other vegetables, water to cover them and salt. Cook for 15 minutes. Add paneer and cook 15 minutes more. Add a little ghee and water as it cooks. You should use approximately 5 tablespoons of ghee altogether. Serve, while hot, with rice or whole wheat toast.

Khoya

This is used as an ingredient in other recipes, like ice cream. It seems like a lot of stirring, but the ice cream that results tastes like it had a lot of energy put into it.

For 1-1½ cups, take ½ gallon MILK and pour into wok. Put on medium to high flame and let it come to a boil. Lower heat and let cook until the water boils out, stirring continuously to prevent scorching which will ruin the taste. When the water has all evaporated and the consistency is that of a very thick custard, it is ready to use.

Tofu (Soy Cheese)

In China it's called "meat without a bone." It's high quality protein.

Soak 1 cup SOY BEANS in enough water to cover for 10 hours. Put 6 cups water in large, stainless steel cooker and bring to boil. Put 2½ cups water in smaller cooker and heat. In blender liquefy half the beans with 1½ cups water and add to large cooker. Repeat with remaining beans. When this boils up in pot, turn off heat. Strain into large saucepan through collander lined with cheesecloth. Put pulp from cheesecloth into water in small cooker. Strain again and press out all milk from pulp. Use a jar or potato masher to press. Rinse large cooker and pour soy milk back into it and boil for 5-7 minutes. Stir often enough to prevent scorching. Meanwhile, thoroughly dissolve 1 teaspoon *nigari** in 1 cup hot water. Add 1/3 solution to boiling milk and stir well from bottom. (Burner may now be turned off.) Stir lightly about 1 inch down from top. Pour another 1/3 solution on top and stir as before. Cover and let stand for 3 minutes. Remove cover, stir lightly on top again. Add last 1/3 solution and stir top once more. Cover and let stand for 3 more minutes. Milk should be well curdled and whey a clear yellow (not milky). Line pressing box† with damp cheesecloth and gently pour curds through cloth. Put top on box and press with weight until cheese is desired consistency. Turn cheese into cold water. It is best when fresh, but may be kept refrigerated under water up to a week, if water is changed twice a day.

---

* A solidifier prepared from seawater. Epsom salts can be substituted, though three times as much is required (about 3 teaspoons in 1 cup hot water for this recipe).

† Available as part of tofu kits.

Tofu Cheese Cake

We couldn't decide whether this should go under beans, dairy or sweets since it's each of those, but it's so good we almost put in under all three.

Prepare the following:
  Crush 1½ cups GRAHAM CRACKERS. (Granola may be used instead.)
Have on hand:
  ¼ - 1/3 cup GHEE
  1½-2 cups TOFU or bean curd (packed)*
  5 tablespoons LIGHT HONEY
  2 EGG YOLKS
  2 tablespoons RAISINS
  4 pitted DATES
  1 tablespoon SESAME BUTTER or TAHINI
  2 tablespoons melted, cooled BUTTER
  ½ teaspoon VANILLA
  ⅛ teaspoon SALT
  7 teaspoons LEMON JUICE
Topping:
  ½ cup SOY MILK
  1 tablespoon granular lecithin (optional)
  ¼ cup GHEE or oil

  Mix crushed graham crackers and ghee and put in pyrex or stainless steel pie plate. Spread to form a crust. Put in 350° oven

---

* Tofu (the most common, Japanese version) may be soft while bean curd (sold in Chinese stores) is drier and stiffer. We use homemade tofu and make it to suit the dish in which we plan to use it. The softer version makes a custardy pie which is creamy, but difficult to serve!

and bake for 10 minutes. Set aside to cool. Put tofu and honey in blender. Blend until smooth and then add egg yolks, raisins, dates, sesame butter, melted butter, vanilla and salt. Blend until smooth and add lemon juice. Blend again. Pour into crust.

Topping, if desired:

Put soy milk in blender. (Granular lecithin is optional.) Turn on medium-high speed and slowly add ¼ cup ghee and blend. If it doesn't thicken, place in refrigerator until it thickens and then spread on top of cheese cake.

Variation: Add ¾ cup paneer* to the tofu. Richer and creamier.

* See recipe for paneer on page 150.

Scrambled Tofu

It looks like scrambled eggs and tastes like scrambled eggs except maybe it's a little better.

Prepare the following:
    Cube 2/3 cup tofu.
    Cube 1/3 cup paneer.
Have on hand:
    1 tablespoon GHEE
    ¼ teaspoon TURMERIC
    ⅛ teaspoon GROUND CUMIN
    ¼ teaspoon GROUND CORIANDER
    ¼ teaspoon SALT
    ½ cup WATER

Put ghee in a heavy, iron frypan and heat on medium flame. Add turmeric, cumin and coriander and fry until brown. Add the tofu and fry until covered with spices. Next add paneer and salt (to taste) and fry till seasonings are evenly distributed. Add about ½ cup water, cover tightly and let cook for about 3 minutes. Remove lid and if still watery, let cook till "broth" is thick and creamy. Serve like scrambled eggs with whole wheat toast, and enjoy.

Variation: In ghee, fry 1 tablespoon grated onion until it begins to brown. Add ⅛ teaspoon turmeric, 1 tablespoon soy sauce or tamari, ¼ teaspoon salt. Mix well, add tofu and water, and cook as above.

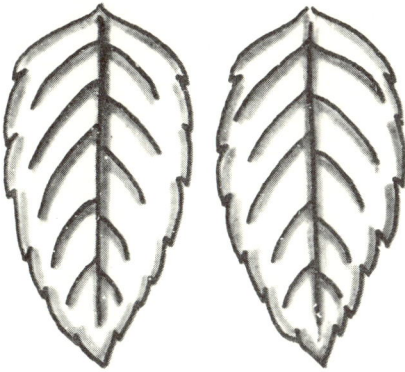

X

Relishes
Chutneys
and Raitas

X Relishes, Chutneys & Raitas

If your meal is dahl and rice with a vegetable made in a heavy sauce, you may want something lighter to perk up the meal. For this purpose, Indians use a variety of relishes, chutneys and yogurt-based dishes which are called raita. They are mostly spicy, but need not be so much so. The mountain sages warn against pickles and relishes made with vinegar and the eating of too much "embalmed" food. But fresh chutneys can be made from green things and lemon juice. There is also a variety of ways of adding vegetables and spices to yogurt so that it becomes a peppy little side dish.

A *raita* or fresh chutney is very much like a ground up salad, and is chocked full of vitamins and minerals.

About 20 minutes
(If yogurt already made)

Serves 8

Raita

A perky sort of yogurt dish that goes nicely with an Indian meal.

Prepare the following:
  3 cups YOGURT*
  Dice or grate 1 six-inch CUCUMBER. (If seeds are large, cut
    out and discard) and soak in salt water (1 teaspoon salt to 1
    cup water).
Have on hand:
  2 teaspoons GROUND CUMIN
  SALT and BLACK PEPPER

  Put ground cumin in a dry frypan and fry until it's dark
brown. Be sure not to let it burn or cook until it's black. Add this
to the yogurt. Then drain the cucumbers and add. Next add salt
and pepper to taste. Some prefer it fairly hot; make it to suit your
taste. Serve with dahl, rice and subzi to include yogurt in the
meal. It's very tasty.

---

* For details see recipe on page 149.

Picku's Chutney

Very tasty served with dahl. Really gives it a great tang.

Prepare the following:
   1 cup fresh MINT LEAVES
   ¾ inch wedge from medium ONION
   juice of ½ LEMON
   ¾ medium GREEN PEPPER
   5 PEPPER CORNS
   ⅛ teaspoon RED PEPPER
   ¼ teaspoon SALT

   Place all ingredients in blender and blend until finely chopped. Ready to serve.

Quick Chutney to serve with Doshas

Good for eating with doshas, or spicing up any meal that's too heavy and lacking in tart, green, zippy flavor. Use your imagination.

Have on hand:
    GREEN PEPPERS
    LEMON JUICE
    FRESH SPINACH
    CAYENNE PEPPER
    BLACK PEPPER
    ½ TOMATO

In a blender throw some green peppers, some lemon juice, a few leaves of spinach or other green vegetable, a little bit of cayenne pepper and a pinch (or two) of black pepper. A half tomato or so can be added and the whole thing chopped in the blender until it's a mushy but not liquid consistency. Doshas dipped in this are quite delicious (see recipe for doshas, page 108).

Apple Chutney

If you have some of this on hand, you can always spice up any meal that needs it. It's a ginger-apple flavor with cinnamon and cloves. It's fun and tickles your nose.

Prepare the following:
Peel, core and mince 3 large APPLES
Squeeze juice of ½ LEMON
Have on hand:
1½ cups APPLE JUICE
½ cup RAW SUGAR
1/3 cup WHITE RAISINS (kishmish)
2 inches fresh mature GINGER ROOT, grated
18 CHUARA* (corrugated dates from Afghanistan), boiled
whole and chopped small
2 large pinches of SALT
⅜-½ cup HONEY

Mince apples, squeezing juice of lemon over them while mincing to prevent them from turning dark and also to flavor them. Boil apples in apple juice. To this add raw sugar, white raisins, ginger root, dates and salt. Cook until apples are tender and sugar is dissolved. Then turn off heat. While hot, but not cooking, add honey. This is like a sweet relish. Very tasty. It will not keep for a long period of time, so be sure to refrigerate.

* Chuara can be purchased in most Indian grocery stores.

XI

Beverages and Soups

XI Beverages & Soups

In India it's uncommon to drink with the meal. In the hot areas, however, plenty of beverages are necessary to cope with the heat, though they are seldom served ice cold as they are in the West.

In the colder areas and in winter time hot liquids are treasured, since heating is minimal. Tea is a favorite, though hot water is considered quite delicious. Hot water with a little lemon and honey is also quite good. And according to the ancient teachings of the mountains it is a most healthful way to warm up on a cold morning.

Tea has been maligned in the West because of its caffeine content. But experiments suggest that it is not harmful in the ways that coffee is. Coffee is also native to India, but has never enjoyed the popularity and high regard that tea has. Tea is high in manganese, a necessary mineral which is missing in many commercially cultivated farmlands in the West. Manganese deficiency has been thought to be connected with nervous problems.

In India tea is never taken with the meal. One might think this is simply a matter of custom, but current research has shown that while it creates no such problems taken alone, tea prevents iron absorption when it is drunk with food. Indian tea is among the best in the world. And it was from India that tea spread to China, where it became quite a national drink. In India, however, tea is often made with milk. This seems to "mellow out" the effect of the caffeine, and at the same time reduce some of the mucous tendencies of the milk. This happy marriage of tea and milk we have come to call, in English, "tilk." It's a popular dairy drink in the mountains, as in much of northern India. (See recipe for tilk.)

If you have considered that tea might be better for your health than coffee, but have never been fond of tea, at least give yourself a chance by trying a good quality tea. Most American brand commercial teas contain the poorest quality tea leaves, which contain dyes and other substances that detract from the taste. If tea is made with a city water supply, which is contaminated with chlorine and other additives, one cannot expect it to be delicious.

Milk shakes are not unknown in India. And the mango milkshake is a delight. Mangos and milk, like bananas and milk, are considered by the mountain people to be a complete diet.

Fruit juices are also enjoyed, especially citrus juices. In the mountains a drink is made from apricots, which is highly regarded for its health-giving qualities.

Tilk

Almost a meal in itself. A welcome lift.

Have on hand:
  1 quart MILK
  1 teaspoon TEA per cup
  HONEY to taste
  CINNAMON (optional)

In the bottom of a stainless steel, two-quart pot put about ¼ of an inch of water. Turn on the heat and as the water begins to boil, pour in milk. Let the milk come to a boil. When it boils up, turn off the heat and dump in one teaspoon of good quality tea for each cup that you wish to make. Then cover. Allow to steep at least 10 minutes. Strain into cups and serve, sweetening with honey. If the honey is too dark, it might overpower the taste of the tea. A dash of cinnamon on top of each cup is sometimes nice for variety. This will make four or five cups.

Tea bags may be used, and they are convenient here since they save you the straining. However, it is said that the tea does not brew as well this way, since it can't "breathe."

Indian Style Tea

Very tasty, but not as rich as tilk. Some may prefer it. The French would probably call it tea "au lait."

Have on hand:
1 teaspoon (level) TEA for each cup of tea desired
BOILING WATER
BOILING MILK
HONEY or SUGAR to taste.

Bring to a boil about a quart of pure water. If your tap water is not good, use bottled water. Have on hand a teapot that will hold at least a pint, or a pint and a half. Pour a bit of the boiling water into this and let it sit until the pot is warm. Empty this water and add 1 teaspoon (level) of tea for each cup you wish to make. Especially recommended are Darjeeling tea and Nilgiris. Indians commonly use a tea which is less fine but full-bodied and quite good when served this way.*

Now pour on top of the tea enough water to make the number of cups you wish. Cover the pot and let it sit for at least ten minutes undisturbed. If it can be in a warm place, that's better. If you don't have a teapot, you can use the pot you boil water in, as long as it's stainless steel, porcelain, or glass; but it should definitely be covered. Pour equal amount of boiling milk into a ceramic pitcher and serve the tea and milk together. Let each person pour as much tea and as much milk as he wishes. Usual proportions are half and half. The tea should be quite dark, since it will be diluted by the milk. It can then be sweetened with sugar, raw sugar or honey. We prefer honey.

* The popular brand is called "Brook Bond, Red Label" available in Indian import stores.

Spiced Tilk

Just imagine a delicious remedy! That's what this is besides being a most tasty treat.

Have on hand:
- 8-10 whole BLACK PEPPER CORNS
- 1 small light CARDAMOM, shelled
- 1 stick CINNAMON, broken up
- ½ inch GINGER ROOT pounded (or one teaspoon of dried ginger root, ground)
- 1 CLOVE
- 1 quart MILK
- 5 teaspoons good quality TEA
- HONEY to taste

In a two-quart pot put an inch to 1½ inches of pure water. Throw in peppercorns, white cardamom, cinnamon, ginger root and clove. Bring to a boil and allow it to boil down to half its volume. Then pour in milk and allow it to come to a boil again. Now put in tea, cover, and allow to steep for 10 minutes. Strain into cups and serve sweetened with honey. This is most warming and invigorating in wintertime. It is also especially helpful in preventing illness if one has been chilled and feels he is about to come down with a cold.

Mango Milkshake

If you can obtain fresh, properly ripened, mangos and a very light crystallized natural honey, then you should definitely try this. You will discover it is the closest thing to heaven that can be put in a glass.

Have on hand:
    Fresh, ripe MANGO
    1½ cups cold (previously boiled) MILK
    1½ tablespoons LIGHT HONEY

Slice mango over a bowl to catch any juice produced during cutting. Spoon mango from skin. Put in blender ½ cup mango, 1½ cups cold milk and 1½ tablespoons light honey. Blend until well mixed. Taste and, if needed, add some of the mango juice or more honey and blend again. Serve.

Cooked Tomato Juice

It's not soup and it's not juice; it's somewhere in between. Often served in a cup to guests while they are waiting for the meal.

Prepare the following:
   Scald, peel and liquify in blender enough fresh TOMATOES
   to make 2 cups juice.
   Chop fine 1 medium ONION.
Have on hand:
   1/3 stick BUTTER
   ½ teaspoon TURMERIC
   1½ teaspoons GROUND CORIANDER
   1 teaspoon GROUND CUMIN
   ½ teaspoon BLACK MUSTARD SEED
   ¼ cup MILK

   Prepare fresh tomato juice. Heat butter in wok on medium flame. Add turmeric, coriander, cumin and fry until brown. Then add mustard seed and fry until brown and seeds begin to pop. Add onion and fry until translucent. Add the tomato juice and rinse blender with milk and pour into wok. Simmer covered until it boils up. Then serve 15-30 minutes before meal.

Variation: Add a 1-inch square of cassia leaf* and simmer for 5-10 minutes; then remove leaf. Serve.

---

* Can be purchased at most Indian grocery stores.

XII
Sweet Dishes

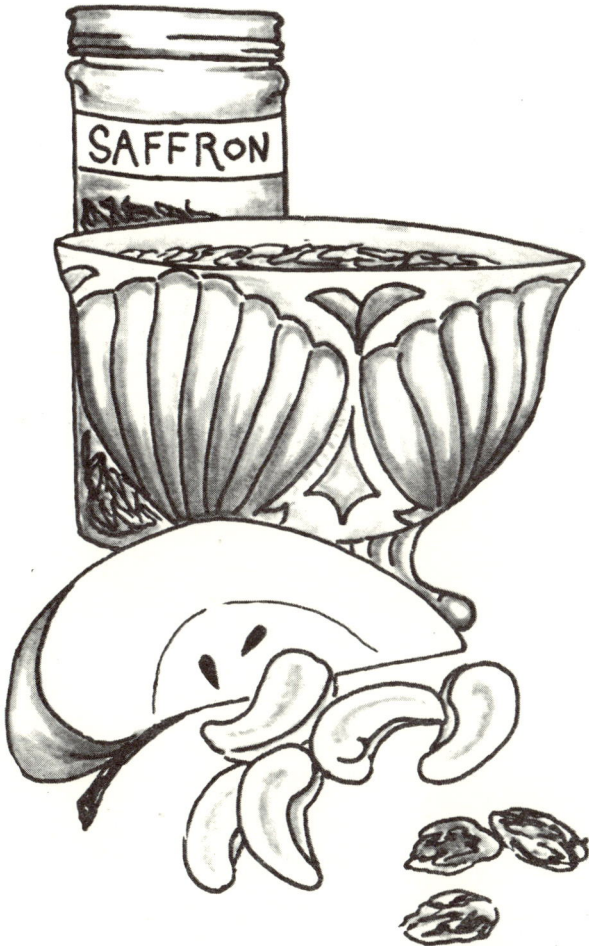

XII Sweet Dishes

Indian sweets are famous the world over. Sugar cane originated in India, and until the present century, honey was quite plentiful, as it still is in the mountains. The delicate flavors of Indian spices, which grow on the steppes of the Himalayan range, are famous the world over, and their delicate aromas have been used to create the masterpieces of Himalayan Mountain confectionery.

Though Indian sweets are shamefully sweet, and often contain huge amounts of sugar, it should be borne in mind that they are not considered part of the daily menu. They are reserved for special occasions such as religious holidays and festivals, and their sweetness is considered symbolic. Tiny pieces of sweets are often distributed by spiritual teachers as *prasad* to their students and in many villages it is the swami that keeps the temple who prepares the sweets that are sold at the entrance way.

The two basic sweet dishes in Indian cookery are halwa and kheer. Kheer is based on rice and is delicate, light and mild. It's nourishing but easy to digest and a favorite of swamis and sadhus who don't want their minds clouded by heavy food. Halwa, by contrast, tends to be a bit heavier, but there are many varieties, each made with its own base. Almost anything can be made into halwa if it is ground up, fried in ghee, and cooked in water or milk with a sweetener. Of course the most common base for halwa is wheat, and it is the least expensive. But halwa is also made from carrots, pumpkins, mung beans and even sesame seeds (as it is in the Middle East). All sorts of goodies are added, like nuts, raisins and so forth and it may be flavored with cardamom, if you wish. (Note: in halwa and kheer recipes, you may wish to substitute honey for raw sugar. If so, add it after cooking, but when the dish is still warm.)

Kheer

Of all the sweet dishes this is considered the most sattvic. It has a delicate flavor and is very light.

Prepare the following:

    Clean and soak ½ cup good quality RICE (e.g. basmati) 2 to 4 hours.

    Heat 2½ quarts MILK.

    Heat 3¾ cups WATER.

    Measure ¼ cup RAW SUGAR. (See note, p. 182.)

    Put 1 dozen strands SAFFRON or seeds from 6-8 cardomom pods (powdered in mortar) in ⅛ cup warm water and let stand 10 minutes.

    Measure ¼ cup RAISINS.

    Chop 1 tablespoon RAW CASHEWS.

Have on hand:

    3 tablespoons GHEE

Heat ghee in wok over medium flame. Add sugar and carmelize slightly. Pour in drained rice and raisins. Fry, stirring with wooden spoon for approximately 3 minutes. It should be gently and slowly fried. Not a single grain should be left out when stirring because if it burns it will ruin the taste. Add 2 cups of milk and the saffron, being careful so that it does not splash out and burn you. When it cooks down and hisses as stirred, add 2 cups milk. Let cook down again as before and add more milk. Stir enough to prevent sticking. Continue this process adding cashews with last milk. It must cook until the rice is very tender and has the consistency of a thick, creamy soup. It must be removed from the flame when it boils and starts popping out of the pot. Serve hot or cold.

Soy Milk Kheer

A soy variation of an old favorite.

Prepare the following:
  Soak 1 cup SOYBEANS overnight. Wash and add fresh water when you can.
Have on hand:
  2 cups BOILING WATER
  1/3 cup RAW SUGAR (See note, p. 182.)
  3 quarts MILK
  ½ cup BASMATI RICE, cleaned and washed in cool water
  ¼ cup WHITE RAISINS
  2 tablespoons broken CASHEWS
  4 tablespoons GHEE.

Drain and put 1 cup soaked beans into blender with 2 cups water. Blend until beans are liquified. Put large strainer into large pot and line strainer with cheesecloth or thin dish cloth. Pour liquified beans into cloth and squeeze until all liquid comes out of beans. (Pulp may be discarded or put aside to be used later.) Now put liquid, or milk, into another pot and add 2 cups of boiling water. (You should use 1 quart of water to each cup of soaked beans.) Add raw sugar to this quart of soy milk and put on very low flame to slowly heat. Now use the other beans in the same manner. You should have approximately 3 quarts of milk altogether.

Put ghee in wok and place on medium to medium-high flame. Add rice and fry for 3 minutes. Be sure to stir carefully so each grain will fry. Add raisins and about 1 pint of soy milk. Let cook until most of the moisture has evaporated. Then add another pint of soy milk and let cook down again. Be sure to stir often. If some browns on bottom scrape off into kheer. This adds flavor. Be sure it doesn't scorch or burn because this will ruin the taste. Continue in this manner letting it cook down each time after adding a pint of milk until the 3 quarts of milk are used. When adding the last pint of milk, add cashews. When most of the moisture has evaporated and the kheer begins to shine as if ghee is coming out, it's ready. Serve immediately.

Apple Date-Nut Halwa

If you make this with apples which are fresh and sweet and crisp, then you'd better make enough for seconds and thirds.

Prepare the following:
    Dissolve 1 cup RAW SUGAR in 1 quart of water.
Have on hand:
    ½ cup GHEE
    ½ cup SOOJI*
    ¼ cup PINE NUTS
    1 large APPLE sliced in ¼ inch slices
    ½ cup DATES, halved

Put pot with sugar and water on burner to heat. In wok put ghee and heat on medium flame. Add sooji and fry until slightly brown. Add the hot sugar water a little at a time, being careful so that it does not pop out and burn you. Cook until very thick and the ghee begins to come out. Add the pine nuts and cook for several minutes. Then add apples and dates. Cook for about 2 minutes. Turn off heat and cover. Apples should be slightly steamed but not cooked. Everything should remain dry and intact. Cut and serve or put in a small dish and serve.

Variation: Use 1 pint of milk in place of 1 quart of water and 1 cup of sooji in place of ½ cup. Use honey in place of raw sugar (see note, p. 182).

* Sooji is a fine cracked wheat similar to cream of wheat but whole grain. Available in most Indian food stores.

Purple Halwa

It's purple if you use fresh pecans and cook it in a steel pot, not stainless steel; but whether it turns purple or not, you'll like it.

Have on hand:
    2 quarts MILK (2% is best)
    1 cup WATER
    ½ cup GHEE
    ½ cup SOOJI*
    1 cup RAW SUGAR (See Note p. 182.)
    ½ cup fresh PECAN HALVES

Put 1 quart milk with ½ cup water in a saucepan and bring to a boil. While the milk boils, put ghee in a wok and heat. Add sooji and fry until golden brown. Now add raw sugar and stir until it begins to melt. Then pour the quart of boiling milk in the wok a little at a time. Be careful so it does not boil out and burn you. Put in pecan halves. In the meantime, put another quart of milk and ½ cup of water in the saucepan and let it come to a boil. Continue to stir the mixture in the wok until it thickens. Then add the quart of boiling milk. Cook until it is very stiff and begins to pull from the sides of the wok, almost pulling the spoon from your hand, and the ghee begins to come out of the halwa. Put it in a plate and let cool. Cut in squares and serve.

* See footnote on page 186.

Mung Halwa

Mung beans are good almost any way; made into halwa, they make a rich, nutty, chewy confection that needs no nuts or raisins. But be warned: a tiny bit is enough.

Have on hand:
   ½ cup WASHED SPLIT MUNG, sorted, washed and
      soaked for several hours
   2 cups WATER
   1½ quarts MILK
   1¼ cups WATER
   1 cup RAW SUGAR (See Note, p. 182.)
   ½ cup GHEE

Put drained and rinsed mung in blender with ¾ cup water and grind until the size of coarse grits. Be careful not to grind too small because halwa will be gummy. Strain and mash out as much water as is possible. (This water may be saved to add to vegetables.) Put milk, sugar and 1½ cups water in a saucepan. Stir until sugar has dissolved. Place on burner to heat.

Put ghee in wok and heat on medium flame. Add mung and fry until light golden brown, stirring very hard and fast until water has cooked out and it looks grainy. If this is not done, the mung will cook into balls and make the halwa lumpy. Add 1 cup of hot liquid and cook until thick, stirring continuously. When it cooks down and spoon makes hissing sound during stirring, add about a cup of hot liquid. Be sure to pull from sides and bottom to prevent sticking. Follow this procedure over and over adding about a cup of milk at a time until all is used. When cooked 1 hour, ghee begins to come out and spoon pulls very hard. Pour halwa into a flat dish to cool. It will stiffen and may be cut and served.

Carrot Halwa

This takes time. Do it on a holiday when you can take turns stirring, and there's not much else to do anyhow. You'll be surprised at what a royal dish the lowly carrot can make.

Prepare the following:

Grate 6-7 CARROTS (about 2½-2¾ cups).

Put 4 cups MILK and ¾ cup RAW SUGAR in saucepan. Stir until sugar has dissolved. Place on medium to low flame and let heat. (To use honey, see note, p. 182.)

Pulverize 1 cup BLANCHED ALMONDS.

Grind seed from 5-6 pods of CARDAMOM.

Have on hand:

¼ cup whole PISTACHIOS

¼ cup GHEE

1 teaspoon ALMOND EXTRACT (or vanilla if preferred)

Put ghee in wok and heat on medium flame. Add grated carrots and fry until as dry as you can get them without burning. Add the hot milk and sugar, being careful that it does not pop out and burn you. Bring to a boil and lower flame and let cook about 10-15 mintues. Add almonds and cook until all water has evaporated, stirring often to prevent sticking and scorching (about 1 hour or more). Then add pistachios, ground cardamom to taste and almond extract. Stir well. Pour into a flat dish and let cool. Cut and serve.

Honey Ice Cream

You'll never want ice cream made with sugar again.

Prepare the following:
    Make ½ gallon whole MILK into Khoya.*
Have on hand:
    ½ gallon whole MILK
    2 cups HEAVY CREAM
    ¾-1 cup LIGHT HONEY (to taste)
    1½ teaspoons VANILLA (optional)

Put ½ gallon whole milk in wok on medium to high flame. Heat, stirring continuously until it boils down to a thick custard consistency (about 1 hour). This is Khoya. Add the other ½ gallon whole milk, heavy cream, honey to taste and vanilla. Mix until well blended. Pour in churn and freeze. Makes about 1 gallon. Serve.

Variation: Add crushed fruit of your choice or nuts sauteed in butter (about ¾-1 cup nuts sauteed in 4-5 tablespoons butter.)

---

* See page 156 for instructions on how to make khoya.

Flavor 34 Ice Cream

When Dr. Misra arrived in America, we already had 33 flavors. He brought "Number 34."

Prepare the following:
Make ½ gallon whole MILK into khoya.*
Have on hand:
    ½ gallon whole MILK
    1/16 teaspoon SAFFRON
    ⅛ cup WATER
    seed from 4 CARDAMOM PODS
    ½ cup CASHEWS
    ¼-⅓ cup PISTACHIOS
    3 BANANAS (blended)
    1 pint WHIPPING CREAM
    ¾ cup LIGHT HONEY

Pour ½ gallon milk in large saucepan (6 quart) and heat on medium flame. When this boils, add saffron which has been crushed in a mortar and soaked in the water. Add the cardamom seed, ground in a mortar. Cook for about 20 minutes. Chop fine the cashews and pistachios and add to saucepan. Turn off heat. Add the bananas, whipping cream, honey and the khoya. Stir and taste. If not sweet enough, add more honey. Put in churn and freeze.

* See page 156 for instructions on how to make khoya.

Glossary

Chapati Flat bread made from whole wheat flour and water.

Chutney Relish made from fresh vegetables or fruit.

Besan Flour made from chick peas or chana dahl.

Dahl An Indian catch-all term which is used for beans, peas, lentils, etc., or a dish made from them.

Dosha A pancake made of ground dahl and rice and fried in ghee.

Halwa An Indian sweet made of dahl, grain or vegetable fried in ghee and cooked in sweetened milk until moisture has evaporated.

Karhi (Curry) A dish made of besan, yogurt and vegetables.

Kheer An Indian sweet made by frying rice in ghee and adding sugar and milk, which is cooked until moisture evaporates, leaving a custardy pudding.

Khichari Rice combined with dahl or vegetables.

Khoya Thick milk made by slowly evaporating water from milk.

Pakori A vegetable dipped in batter made of dahl and fried in hot ghee.

Paneer Cheese made from milk curdled with lemon juice.

Pullao A rice and vegetable dish cooked together so that the flavors mingle.

Raita Diced vegetable in spiced yogurt.

Sag Spinach, mustard greens or other leafy greens.

Subzi Vegetables or a dish made of vegetables.

Tofu Soy cheese (similar to paneer but made from soy milk and curdled with nigari).

Index

A

Adarak (see Ginger), 19-20
Ajwain, 21
Almonds, recipes used in:
    "Chocolate" Dahl, 112-113
    Pakori, 114
    Chana Stew with Nuts,
    118-119
    Himalayan Pizza, 138-139
    Hindu Loaf, 140
    Loaf, 142
    Kheer, 183
    Carrot Halwa, 189
Aluminum pots and pans, 9
Amino acids, 93
Anise seed, 23
Apple Chutney, 167
Apple-Date-Nut Halwa, 186
Apricots, juice, 172
Arahar, 95
Asafoetida, 21
Asparagus, 42
    recipes used in:
    Creamed Vegetable Delight,
    64-65
    Cashew Subzi, 67

B

Bajara Bran Muffins, 132
Bajara Ki Roti, 128
Banana Pepper, recipe used in:
    Garbanzo Stew, 120-121
Basic Mung Dahl, 98

Basic Vegetable (subzi), 46-47
Basmati (rice), 76
    recipes used in:
    "Brown rice," 80
    Picku's Rice, 81
    Khichari, 82
    Fakir Ki Khichari, 86-87
    Green Rice, 88-89
    Picku's Pullao, 90
    Kheer, 183
    Soy Milk Kheer, 184-185
Battwa (Lambs Quarters), 44
    nutritional properties of, 44
Beans, 28, 31, 77 (also see Dahl,
    93)
    Dried, for hemoglobin build-
    up, 93
Besan (see Gram), 94
    recipes using: 114, 118-119
Beverages, 171-172
Black Cardamom, 20
Black Gram (see Urad Dahl), 95
Black pepper, 19
Brass pots, 9
Bread *(roti),* 28, 32, 125-128
    in meal planning, 28
    recipes:
    Chapatis, 129
    Crisp Chapatis, 130
    Paranthas, 131
    Bajara Bran Muffins, 132
    Wheat/Soy Bread, 133
    Oopma, 134-135
    Leaf Cake, 136-137
Breads, types of:

G

H

T

The main building of the national headquarters, Honesdale, Pa.

The Himalayan Institute

The Himalayan International Institute of Yoga Science and Philosophy of the U.S.A. is a nonprofit organization devoted to the scientific and spiritual progress of modern humanity. Founded in 1971 by Sri Swami Rama, the Institute combines Western and Eastern teachings and techniques to develop educational, therapeutic, and research programs for serving people in today's world. The goals of the Institute are to teach meditational techniques for the growth of individuals and their society, to make known the harmonious view of world religions and philosophies, and to undertake scientific research for the benefit of humankind.

This challenging task is met by people of all ages, all walks of life, and all faiths who attend and participate in the Institute courses and seminars. These programs, which are given on a continuing basis, are designed in order that one may discover for oneself how to live more creatively. In the words of Swami Rama, "By being aware of one's own potential and abilities, one can become a perfect citizen, help the nation, and serve humanity."

The Institute has branch centers and affiliates throughout the United States. The 422-acre campus of the national headquarters, located in the Pocono Mountains of northeastern Pennsylvania, serves as the coordination center for all the Institute activities, which include a wide variety of innovative programs in education, research, and therapy, combining Eastern and Western approaches to self-awareness and self-directed change.

SEMINARS, LECTURES, WORKSHOPS, and CLASSES are available throughout the year, providing intensive training and experience in such topics as Superconscious Meditation, hatha yoga, philosophy, psychology, and various aspects of personal growth and holistic health. The *Himalayan News*, a free bimonthly publication, announces the current programs.

The RESIDENTIAL and SELF-TRANSFORMATION PROGRAMS provide training in the basic yoga disciplines— diet, ethical behavior, hatha yoga, and meditation. Students are also given guidance in a philosophy of living in a community environment.

The PROGRAM IN EASTERN STUDIES AND COM-PARATIVE PSYCHOLOGY is the first curriculum offered by an educational institution that provides a systematic synthesis of Western empirical sciences with Eastern introspective sciences using both practical and traditional approaches to education. The University of Scranton, by an agreement of affiliation with the Himalayan Institute, is prepared to grant credits for coursework in this program, and upon successful completion of the program awards a Master of Science degree.

The five-day STRESS MANAGEMENT/PHYSICAL FITNESS PROGRAM offers practical and individualized training that can be used to control the stress response. This includes biofeedback, relaxation skills, exercise, diet, breathing techniques, and meditation.

A yearly INTERNATIONAL CONGRESS, sponsored by the Institute, is devoted to the scientific and spiritual progress of modern humanity. Through lectures, workshops, seminars, and practical demonstrations, it provides a forum for professionals and lay people to share their knowledge and research.

The ELEANOR N. DANA RESEARCH LABORATORY is the psychophysiological laboratory of the Institute, specializing in research on breathing, meditation, holistic therapies, and stress and relaxed states. The laboratory is fully equipped for exercise stress testing and psychophysiological measurements, including brain waves, patterns of respiration, heart rate changes, and muscle tension. The staff investigates Eastern teachings through studies based on Western experimental techniques.

Himalayan Institute Publications

Living with the Himalayan Masters	Swami Rama
Lectures on Yoga	Swami Rama
A Practical Guide to Holistic Health	Swami Rama
Choosing a Path	Swami Rama
Inspired Thoughts of Swami Rama	Swami Rama
Freedom from the Bondage of Karma	Swami Rama
Book of Wisdom (Ishopanishad)	Swami Rama
Enlightenment Without God	Swami Rama
Exercise Without Movement	Swami Rama
Life Here and Hereafter	Swami Rama
Marriage, Parenthood, and Enlightenment	Swami Rama
Perennial Psychology of the Bhagavad Gita	Swami Rama
Emotion to Enlightenment	Swami Rama, Swami Ajaya
Science of Breath	Swami Rama, Rudolph Ballentine, M.D., Alan Hymes, M.D.
Yoga and Psychotherapy	Swami Rama, Rudolph Ballentine, M.D., Swami Ajaya
Superconscious Meditation	Usharbudh Arya, D.Litt.
Mantra and Meditation	Usharbudh Arya, D.Litt.
Philosophy of Hatha Yoga	Usharbudh Arya, D.Litt.
Meditation and the Art of Dying	Usharbudh Arya, D.Litt.
God	Usharbudh Arya, D.Litt.
Psychotherapy East and West: A Unifying Paradigm	Swami Ajaya, Ph.D.
Yoga Psychology	Swami Ajaya, Ph.D.
Foundations of Eastern and Western Psychology	Swami Ajaya (ed.)
Psychology East and West	Swami Ajaya (ed.)
Meditational Therapy	Swami Ajaya (ed.)
Diet and Nutrition	Rudolph Ballentine, M.D.
Joints and Glands Exercises	Rudolph Ballentine, M.D. (ed.)
Freedom from Stress	Phil Nuernberger, Ph.D.
Science Studies Yoga	James Funderburk, Ph.D.